Praise for *The Vanguard Edge*

I love *The Vanguard Edge*. Bryan addresses one of the most important variables for the organization of the future, effective team performance. He shows not only why it matters so much, he teaches leaders how to make it happen!

Marshall Goldsmith | #1 Thinkers50 World Leadership Thinker, World's #1 Executive Coach, and the #1 New York Times Bestselling Author of *What Got You Here Won't Get You There, Triggers,* **and** *The Earned Life*

In my experience at the helm of several firms in the financial services industry, the true test of leadership is in how we build and guide our teams. *The Vanguard Edge* hits the mark on what it takes to lead effectively in our constantly changing business environment. It offers clear, practical advice that resonates with those of us committed to driving real progress and cultivating a winning team culture. A valuable read for leaders at any level.

Rob Clements | Chairman and CEO, Covius Holdings, Inc.

The Vanguard Edge is a much-needed guide to building unparalleled high-performance teams. With his 6M Framework, Bryan provides a clear roadmap for leaders to cultivate teams that go beyond the ordinary and challenge the status quo. From nurturing a growth mindset to creating a convincing voice, each "M" is a building block for success, ensuring teams are not just functional but also visionary. As someone who has witnessed Bryan's expertise, I can attest that this book isn't just theory; it's a practical toolkit born from real-world challenges and experiences. *The Vanguard Edge* is the key to unlocking your team's full potential and gaining the necessary edge in today's ever-changing business landscape.

Ed Roberts | COO, Bozard Ford Lincoln

The Vanguard Edge by Bryan Howard is a compelling guide to masterful team leadership. His 6M Framework is both practical and transformative, filled with real-life insights that resonate with today's leaders. Particularly impactful are his strategies on fostering growth mindsets and resilience within teams. This book is not just a resource but a beacon for those aspiring to elevate their leadership and drive genuine team success. It's a concise, powerful read that I'll be revisiting often for both strategy and inspiration.

Brad Costanzo | CEO, Accelerated Intelligence AI

Bryan Howard's *The Vanguard Edge* is a masterclass in team leadership, offering rich, in-depth knowledge that's both insightful and actionable. Each chapter unfolds new horizons for team growth and synergy. It's the ultimate playbook for anyone committed to driving their team forward.

Blake Wilson | CEO, Monarch Capital Investments

Whether you lead a team of a few or hundreds, *The Vanguard Edge* provides the strategy every business needs to ensure success. Teams who adopt these tools won›t just survive, they›ll thrive and leave powerful legacies.

Laura Di Franco | CEO, Brave Healer Productions

Bryan Howard is a pure visionary who thinks and acts at the highest level. He truly cares about people and lives in full abundance. He is a master of team building as well, and his book provides a simple process for creating and building the best team for your company.

Justin Breen | CEO, BrEpic Network

The Vanguard Edge is not just a book; it's a movement towards peak performance and efficiency. It's more than a book, it's a catalyst for enduring and exponential change for every leader and every organization. Bryan Howard's expertise shines on every page.

Mike Malatesta | Founder, Entrepreneur, Author, and Dream Exit Expert

A transformative guide that redefines the essence of teamwork. *The Vanguard Edge* is a brilliant blend of strategic foresight and actionable intelligence.

Dr. Kathy Humel | CEO, Senior Consultant RxKHumel, LLC

Bryan Howard has crafted a roadmap for success that is both insightful and actionable. This book is essential for anyone serious about leading a team.

Shawn Johal | Business Growth Coach, Elevation Leaders, Bestselling Author of *The Happy Leader*

UNCOVER
Your Leadership Style with The Vanguard Edge

Are you an Aspiring Vanguard, an Emerging Vanguard, or a Vanguard at the helm? Take our free Vanguard Leadership Readiness Quiz to discover your unique leadership qualities and how you can harness them for growth.

Complete the quiz and receive a personalized report that aligns with The Vanguard Edge's powerful insights. Connect your style with our principles and prime yourself for an enriching leadership journey.

Start your assessment now at:
vanguardedge.com/takethequiz
Unlock your leadership potential today!

THE
VANGUARD
EDGE

YOUR
6–STEP METHOD
TO UNPARALLELED
TEAM SUCCESS

Leaders
Press

BRYAN HOWARD

Leaders
Press

ISBN **978-1-63735-272-4** (pbk)
ISBN **978-1-63735-273-1** (ebook)

Library of Congress Control Number: 2023916621

To my wife, Erica, who makes my life infinitely better.
I'm the lucky one.

Contents

Foreword

Bryan Howard's *The Vanguard Edge* is the Future of Team Leadership!

Exceptional leaders and teams are no longer optional for any organization that wants to not only survive, but thrive.

This book is THE blueprint for creating what Bryan calls "Vanguard Teams"—ones that embody a growth mindset, thrive on challenges, and continually push limits through innovation and excellence. His framework revolves around six core components for team success: Mindset, Mission, Model, Message, Metrics, and Multipliers.

Miss any part of this sequence, and you get mediocre results. Nail them all, and your team becomes an unstoppable force.

In this book, Bryan gives you amazing tools to assess your team's current dynamics and strengths. Then, he offers easy to implement resources to instill a winning mindset, define a compelling mission, build an optimized model, craft a clear message, track progress with smart metrics, and leverage multipliers for exponential gains. His step-by-step process transforms groups that may have been stagnant or siloed into ones that are adaptive, energized, and collaborative.

The *Vanguard Edge* is an owner's manual for constructing world-class teams. Bryan doesn't deal in theory. His insights come from decades of real-world application and years perfecting the formula that converts teams from mediocre to magnificent. He distills decades of expertise into a results-driven playbook. One of my favorite elements is a system he created to help teams iterate and celebrate along the way. The Vanguard Edge keeps your team sailing smoothly into the future by ensuring you build on wins, continually upgrade skills, and stay aligned with the overarching company mission.

If you lead a team, belong to a team, or want to build a team, devour this book. The Vanguard Edge delivers the X-factor that multiplies teamwork, maximizes human capital, and accelerates your organization. Boom! Win-Win-Win!

And if you ever have a chance to WORK with Bryan and his team, DO IT!

Mike Koenigs, *Founder of The Superpower Accelerator and co-host of Capability Amplifier podcast*

Introduction

*Great things in business are never done by one person;
they're done by a team of people.*
—Steve Jobs

Teamwork. It seems like everyone talks about it.

"It makes the dream work."

"It divides the task and multiplies the success."

"There is no 'I' in team."

"Talent wins games, but teamwork," as Michael Jordan once noted, "wins championships."

Teamwork in today's business world is not a cliché. It is an imperative. Company leaders who know how to design and motivate high-functioning teams win, and those who create loose teams by merely rearranging the boxes on their org chart don't. It's as simple as that.

Great team environments allow individuals to bring their diverse ideas to problems, increasing the likelihood of an efficient and effective solution. Teams free of corporate hierarchy develop trust and "psychological safety" that fosters creativity, engagement, and innovative solutions. Teams help people learn, cultivate strong working relationships, and heighten your employees' sense of ownership, purpose, and accomplishment. Morale soars. Turnover declines. Profits pile up.

In this age of remote work, teams are as important as ever. Increasingly, companies rely on geographically dispersed workers, and many struggle to make those teams successful. It's harder to build camaraderie when team members can't easily connect and align, and even geographically connected teams can flounder under poor communications, risk aversion, and accountability questions. Leaders often lack the tools they need to pull together great teams with a shared mindset, a clear mission, and the right metrics to measure progress.

This book is designed to address that problem. In it, I explore what I call the 6M Framework, a system for building teams based on mindset, mission, model, message, metrics, and multipliers. The central goal of the 6M Framework is to create a Vanguard team that shares a growth mindset, sets ambitious goals, and follows a structural and operational blueprint that ensures the team's attitude and mission translate into actionable strategies and workflows.

MULTIPLIERS
↑
METRICS
↑
MESSAGE

MUST BE
DONE
IN ORDER

↑
MODEL
↑
MISSION
↑
MINDSET

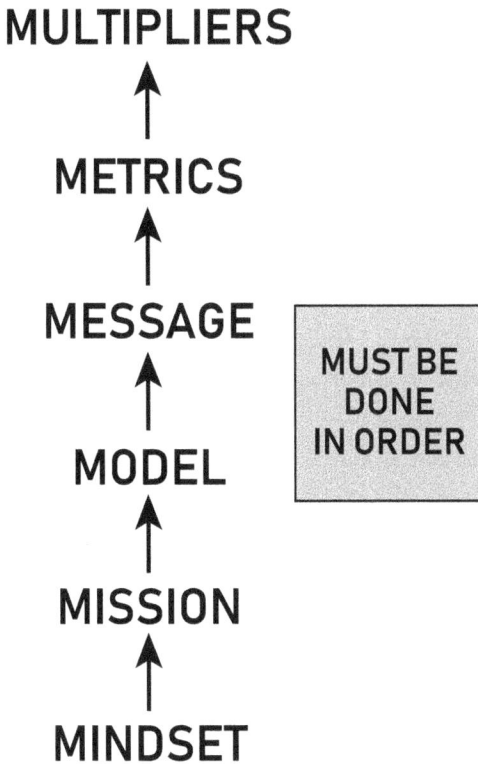

But I don't stop there. The **6M** Framework also explains how Vanguard teams can create a voice and a compelling message that helps them rally support, secure resources, and drive change within and outside the organization. The framework guides leaders in finding the right key performance indicators to measure their team's success. It suggests ways to amplify the team's output, efficiency, or impact through strategic partnerships or other multipliers.

Each chapter that follows dives into each of the Ms in the 6M Framework, starting with how to nurture a growth mindset in teams that may be contentedly stuck in the status quo. The order of the 6Ms is crucial, and implementing them in the correct order is vital to your overall success. The framework—and the tools you need to build that framework—is best assembled in sequence. Each one of these building blocks builds on the previous one, and addressing them in the right order eliminates confusion and ensures your team is ready for its next challenge. In the end, you have a team that is ready for anything. It has the confidence, optimism, structure, cadence, voice, and metrics to tackle your toughest challenges. In fact, it's the kind of team that *anticipates* tough challenges and takes steps to address them before they surface.

It's that kind of a team. A Vanguard team that provides the Vanguard edge!

How should you use this book? While some readers might be tempted to skip ahead ("My team's already got a growth mindset," you might say), I encourage you to take one "M" at a time and in the correct order. If you see no reason to change what you're doing at the end of the first chapter, email me so I can send you a refund. Either that or give the book to someone else, or use it as a coaster on your coffee table.

I don't think you will do that, though. Any leader who has tried to assemble a crack team knows how difficult it can be. It's difficult to find complementary teammates, and it's difficult to keep them operating at a high level. But what you'll find in this book are techniques for creating Vanguard teams and putting them on a path of continuous improvement. Their system for working together, measuring their progress, and celebrating wins ensures the team continues to grow, evolve, and improve, creating a high level of successful operation that will flow throughout your organization.

This book will be your road map, and many of the tools, templates, and assessments you'll need are available on our companion website at no additional charge (www. vanguardedge.com/resources).

Why should you listen to me? With several decades in HR and leadership coaching, I've transformed teams across diverse sectors and company sizes, from start-ups to Fortune 50 companies. As the founder and current CEO of Mercury Performance Group, I've turned challenges into success stories, making a tangible difference in both traditional and remote team dynamics. My insights aren't just theoretical; they're born from real-world experiences. I've been in the trenches, and I've consistently delivered results. My interest in designing a bulletproof approach to teams started many years ago when a large company brought me in as a change agent for a new HR technology. I accomplished a lot during my four years there—except for what they hired me to do. No matter how hard I tried to shift attitudes, the company's risk-aversion and sunk-cost mindset muffled any progress. My team's suggestions were ignored, and the company consistently preferred outside opinions over the expert internal employees they hired to complete the work. Many years, resignations, and new hires later, the work still wasn't complete.

That experience taught me that great teams are built by their members, and they only work if the team has autonomy, diversity, and confidence. Great teams aren't afraid to fail. They learn from their mistakes and continually look for ways to improve. They are agile and persistent. But creating teams like that requires patience, the right attitude, and a methodology ensuring the right implementation.

That's what this book supplies. I'll give you the tools you need to assess your talent, promote the right culture, and ensure your teams remain consistent and productive. The companion toolkit creates momentum where teams keep rolling, keep improving, and keep solving bigger and thornier problems. I'll also share real-world examples of how companies have employed these methods to achieve great success. These stories illustrate the procedures, blueprints, playbooks, and workshops you'll need to overcome obstacles and unhelpful attitudes that can defeat even the best-intentioned teams.

And, as you'll soon see, the process of becoming a Vanguard Team begins with developing the right mindset. That's our first "M," so if you're ready, turn the page and start building your team.

Chapter 1

Mindset: The Foundation of Every High-Performing Team

Whether you think you can, or you think you can't, you're right.
—Henry Ford

Some of you probably remember the BlackBerry, one of the first smartphones. It was introduced in 1999, and by 2013, it had 85 million subscribers. People who owned BlackBerry phones, including me, loved them. They had a small keyboard built into the phone's face, and those who learned "thumbing" could crank out detailed text messages almost as fast as someone using a laptop or PC. Moreover, BlackBerry allowed your messages to be sent over a secure, dependable network, making them a favorite of corporate executives and government officials.

Despite its devoted fans, by 2016, the BlackBerry phone was obsolete—overwhelmed by the popularity of a new generation of smartphones from Apple, Samsung, and others.

Many associate the demise of the BlackBerry with corporate failure, an inability to keep up with the competition.

The company's leaders tried several varieties of flip phones, touchscreens, and sliding covers, but nothing could compete with the iPhones, Galaxies, and other faster, flashier phones flooding the market. It was as if the company leaders decided that thumbing and tiny buttons were the limits of their imagination and ability, so they gave up. By 2022, the BlackBerry was officially "decommissioned" and no longer functional.

What many don't realize, however, is that BlackBerry is still around. In fact, it's flourishing. Security was always the company's main strength, and today, it has transformed itself into a cybersecurity juggernaut, securing more than 500 million endpoints in the Internet of Things, including nearly 200 million vehicles. In May 2022, the retooled BlackBerry Limited company reported almost $170 million in revenue in the first quarter of the fiscal year. Loser? Doesn't sound like it to me.

What helped BlackBerry turn the corner was the growth mindset of its company leaders. These leaders refused to see limitations for their company, but instead believed that with persistence and focused work, they could overcome their challenges and reignite their company. They had the confidence to transform themselves. They are what I call a Vanguard team.

What Is a Vanguard Team?

A Vanguard team is built on trust, a growth mindset, and an innate, proactive vision. They don't see an event, setback, challenge, or defeat as something that's destroying them or something they have to accept. Instead, they see it as an opportunity to move forward in some new way, even when they aren't sure what the path is yet. What's vital is that Vanguard teams anticipate these events, allowing them to acknowledge setbacks and react to them quickly. Because the team is built on trust by the members, team members aren't afraid to say what's on their minds, bring ideas to the table, and resolve the problem. They don't mind inventing and iterating. The solution doesn't have to be perfect. It just has to be progress.

The Kübler-Ross Change Curve, developed by Elisabeth Kübler-Ross, charts the stages individuals experience when facing significant change or loss. Initially designed to understand emotions in terminally ill patients, it's now widely applied in various contexts, including as a "resilience curve" in business transitions. It starts with shock or denial that a business disruption has occurred, then moves to anger or protest. When flustered and defeated business leaders realize the situation isn't going to change, they start bargaining and looking for new ways to fit into the disrupted reality. Eventually, they begin to accept (more often acquiescing than accepting) the disruption and finally turn their attention to fixing their new problem.

RESILIENCE CURVE COMPARISON

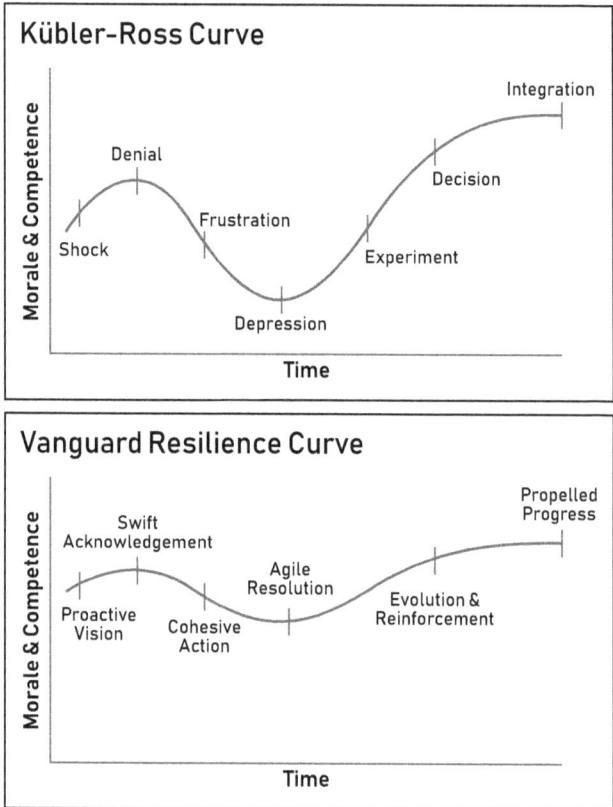

Kübler-Ross Curve

Vanguard Resilience Curve

The resilience curve for a Vanguard team—we call it VRC, the Vanguard Resilience Curve—is quite different. It starts with a proactive vision, moves to swift acknowledgment, and then to cohesive action and agile resolution. The fifth stage of the curve is defined by evolution and adaptation, followed by propelled progress. In other words, you turn up the gas once you find your new path. See the difference? In the traditional resilience curve, your team has to go through four stages before confronting the problem. With Vanguard team resilience, you're addressing the problem before it even arises so you're ready to respond immediately.

The Growth Mindset

In her 2006 book, *Mindset: The New Psychology of Success*, Stanford psychologist Carol Dweck describes the difference between a fixed mindset and a growth mindset. A fixed mindset believes abilities are static and can't be changed. The fixed-mindset person avoids challenges. They say things like, "I'm just not good at math," or "I wish I could do that." Some people think they aren't cut out for entrepreneurship, for instance, when, in fact, entrepreneurial skills can be learned and improved, just like any other skill.

The growth mindset believes intelligence, abilities, and talents can be developed through dedication and hard work. You don't believe in inherent limitations, but instead believe you can gain the skills and knowledge you need to excel. Every challenge is a learning opportunity. Failure isn't bad; it's just a springboard for future success.

Here's an example that illustrates the difference between these two mindsets: Let's say your company is presented with a merger opportunity with a rival company. The fixed mindsets on your leadership team will say, "Mergers are risky. We might lose our company culture." The growth mindsets on the team sing a different tune: "The merger could open up new markets and synergies. Let's evaluate the pros and cons." Exact same situation. Two different approaches.

In today's fast-paced business climate, where customers expect instant results and new companies emerge and fold at lightning speed, a growth mindset is the crucial difference between companies that soar and those that sink. Incorporating the principles of a growth mindset into your leadership team allows your company to thrive—to learn, innovate, and push boundaries.

A growth mindset can deliver tangible, measurable improvements in performance and results. A mindset that embraces innovation leads to improved problem-solving and stronger competitiveness. Teams with a growth mindset are nimble and tenacious; they turn failures into opportunities.

As we suggested earlier, Vanguard teams are rich in the growth mindset. Most CEOs likely already know which individuals on their team have a growth mindset, but to determine the team's mindset as a whole, I've developed the Mindset and Strength Evaluation Tool (MSET). It rates your team's strengths (from weak to strong) and mindset (from fixed to growth on a spectrum). The assessment has thirty questions. Your team's score will determine its place in one of four quadrants. (See accompanying illustration).

MSET TEAM QUADRANTS

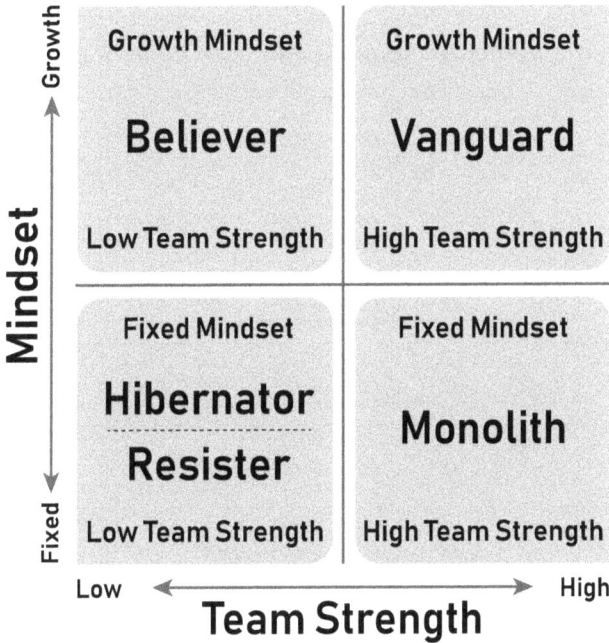

	Growth Mindset	Growth Mindset
Growth ↑	**Believer**	**Vanguard**
	Low Team Strength	High Team Strength
	Fixed Mindset	Fixed Mindset
↓ **Fixed**	**Hibernator** ‑ ‑ ‑ ‑ ‑ ‑ **Resister**	**Monolith**
	Low Team Strength	High Team Strength

Mindset

Low ← → High

Team Strength

As you can see, the place to be is in the upper right quadrant, the Vanguard team. The bottom right quadrant is for Monoliths and comprises high-performing but fixed-mindset teams. The upper left quadrant is for Believers, and it's for weak teams with a growth mindset. The bottom left quadrant is divided into two sections. The top section is for what we call Hibernators, and the bottom is for Resistors.

Finding out where your team lands is the first question. But the overarching, prevailing question is this: Whatever my team is now, how can I get them to become a Vanguard team? How can I create a super team? The goal of this book—and of the hands-on training this book is based on—is to teach you how to do that.

When leaders are skeptical about the value of a growth mindset, I pose four simple questions:

- Would you like your team to be more innovative and creative?

- Would you like them to be more resilient and better able to handle setbacks?

- Do you want them to be more adaptable and agile in the face of change?

- Do you want them to be more engaged, motivated, and committed to their work?

If you answer "yes" to any of those questions, you're more committed to the idea of building a Vanguard team than you may have thought. Each question states the value of a growth mindset and helps even skeptical leaders envision the value of a Vanguard team.

Once leaders understand the "why" behind a Vanguard team—teams that are more innovative, creative, resilient, etc.—we provide them with key action steps to help their Monoliths, Believers, Hibernators, and Resisters move into that vaunted Vanguard quadrant.

For example, how do you move a Monolith group? A Monolith is characterized by high team strength and a fixed mindset. They prefer the status quo, resist change, don't like taking risks, and rely on hierarchical structures and top-down decision-making. For these folks, you'd want to invest in leadership development emphasizing a growth mindset, implement constructive and solution-oriented feedback loops, and give team members opportunities to upskill and reskill. See the accompanying section, Assessing Your Team's Mindset and Strength, at the end of this chapter, for more details on the four quadrants and how to move teams toward the Vanguard quadrant.

Regardless of what type of team you start with, you're the leader. Your role in convincing them to change and improve is paramount. A lot of it has to do with persuasion. Just as the four questions above gave you a strong reason to transform your team, your team members will also respond better if you offer them a compelling vision for the end state and continually remind them of that vision and why you're working toward it.

Still, you may lose some people. Some people just won't want to make that journey with you. You'll ask others to leave. But if you have a vision for the end state and continually communicate it, most people will follow you. In business, you have to give your team members a way to grow, a chance to show, and a place to go.

Nurturing a Team Culture That Breeds Success

To build a Vanguard team, you need a strong foundation. To provide that, I've designed a set of building blocks called the Vanguard Foundation Framework that anyone can use to build their team. The building blocks, in this order, include the following:

- Trust and safety

- Clear communication and role clarity

- Shared vision and purpose

- Collaborative processes and tools

- Continuous learning and adaptability

- Collective achievement and recognition

Each of these building blocks corresponds to one or more of the Ms in the 6M Framework we discussed in the framework. In this chapter, we've focused on the value of mindset—you have to have a growth mindset to adopt these principles. In future chapters, we explore the remaining five Ms so that by the end of the book, you've implemented all 6 Ms and have your Vanguard team.

VANGUARD FOUNDATION FRAMEWORK

Building Blocks of a Thriving Team Culture

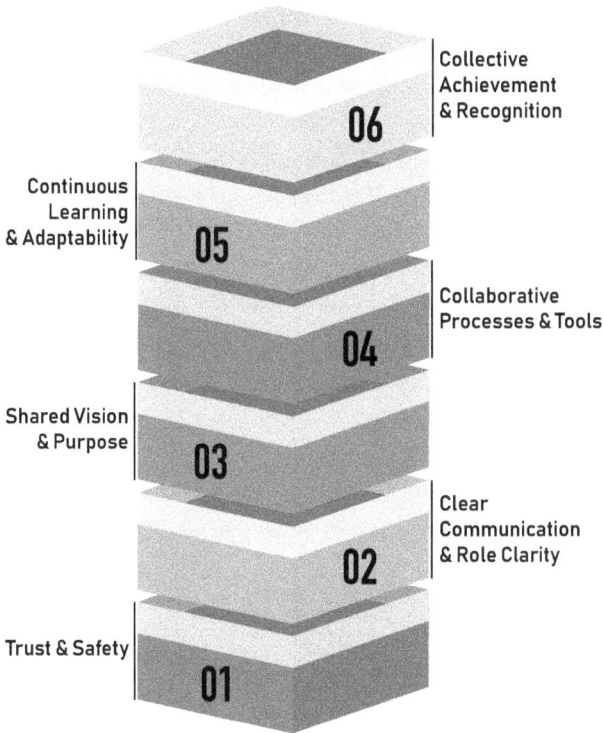

06 — Collective Achievement & Recognition

05 — Continuous Learning & Adaptability

04 — Collaborative Processes & Tools

03 — Shared Vision & Purpose

02 — Clear Communication & Role Clarity

01 — Trust & Safety

This is not an overnight process. It takes time. Remember, there are six steps to the **6M Framework** for High-Performance Teams—mindset, mission, model, message, metrics, and multipliers—and each step builds on the previous ones. It's a journey, an iterative process, and you'll likely make some mistakes along the way. That's okay. Remember, Vanguard teams are better able to handle setbacks, so keep moving forward despite a few missteps along the way.

Getting Started

Again, it all starts with mindset. If you adopt a growth mindset, the rest of the Ms will fall into place over time.

As noted earlier, it also starts with the MSET assessment. The assessment includes fifteen statements about team strength and fifteen about growth mindset. Participants rate each statement on a scale from 1 to 5, with 1 being the worst and 5 being the best. The statements address the team as a whole, not as individual members. Each team member completes the assessment of the whole team, and then those answers are averaged into a composite score. The team leader does their own assessment of the team, which results in a separate score.

I designed this book and the companion website so that teams of all types, levels, and sizes can benefit from *The Vanguard Edge*. The information and tools you need to create a Vanguard team are on these pages, or provided for no additional cost on our website. You only need to bring the grit necessary to see the process through despite the challenges you'll encounter on the way to success. Nothing worth doing is easy.

We also have an option for a three-day, done-for-you workshop, where I or one of our Vanguard experts leads you and your team through the process. As pre-work before that workshop, participants provide answers to some additional questions. We aggregate that data, and then the workshop facilitator assesses the team to produce a separate MSET score. In the end, we can say, "This is how the leader views the team. This is how the team views itself. And based on the team's answers to the supplement questions, this is how we view the team. Every ninety days, everyone does a reassessment to see if there is any movement toward the rarified air of the upper right Vanguard team quadrant.

When you look at BlackBerry's journey from a fixed-mindset team to a strong, growth-mindset team, you can see how the company—under the leadership of John Chen—pivoted from a Monolith team to a Vanguard team. They were being crushed in the phone business but used the same building blocks we've outlined here to become one of the top SaaS companies in the world. The story of that journey should be enough to convince any leader in business to adopt the principles we outline in these pages.

Anyone can do what BlackBerry did. It took several years, and they lost some people through the resilience curve. But in the end, they had an amazing story to tell.

Key Takeaways

- Vanguard teams view setbacks (or even outright defeats) as an opportunity to move forward in a new way. Moreover, they often anticipate setbacks, which allows them to react quickly. Debate among team members is open and honest, allowing all ideas to be expressed and for problems to be rapidly identified and solved.

- Vanguard teams follow a brisk resilience curve. Instead of following a traditional resilience curve, which wastes time with shock, denial, anger, and bargaining, Vanguard teams jump right to swift acknowledgment, cohesive action, and agile resolution.

- A growth mindset is crucial in today's fast-paced business climate. It allows your team to learn, innovate, and push boundaries, while quickly meeting customer's expectations. A growth mindset fosters tangible improvements and results, improving your team's problem-solving and competitiveness. Growth mindset teams turn failures into opportunities.

Assessing Your Team's Mindset and Strength

The Mindset and Strength Evaluation Tool (MSET) measures team strength (how well team members help, trust, and support each other), adaptability (their ability to pivot and learn from mistakes), innovation and problem-solving, openness to feedback, and commitment to personal and collective growth.

You can access the MSET at no additional cost on the companion website at www.vanguardedge.com/resources.

It consists of thirty statements, each with a numerical rating of 1 to 5, and the statements are divided equally between mindset and team strength. The highest score for each is 75.

Here's how to interpret the scores:

- Team strength
    - 15 to 44: low team strength
    - 45 to 75: high team strength

- Mindset
    - 15 to 44: fixed mindset
    - 45 to 75: growth mindset

Quadrant Characteristics

Vanguards—High Team Strength and Growth Mindset

- **Adaptable.** Vanguards quickly adjust to changes and see challenges as opportunities for growth.

- **Collaborative.** They work seamlessly together, valuing each member's input and expertise.

- **Innovative.** Always seeking new ways to improve and optimize. They're at the forefront of industry trends.

- **Continuous learners.** They invest in personal and team development, always looking to expand their knowledge and skills.

- **Solution-oriented.** Instead of dwelling on problems, they focus on finding and implementing solutions efficiently.

Believers—Low Team Strength and Growth Mindset

- **Optimistic.** Even when faced with setbacks, Believers remain hopeful and believe in their potential.

- **Open to feedback.** They actively seek feedback to improve, even if their current team dynamics aren't strong.

- **Willing to change.** They recognize their weaknesses and are willing to make necessary changes.

- **Eager to learn.** While they may lack some skills or knowledge, they're eager to learn and grow.

- **Resilient.** They bounce back from challenges, driven by their belief in a better future.

Monoliths—High Team Strength and Fixed Mindset

- **Efficient.** Monoliths have established processes that they execute well, leading to strong team performance.

- **Resistant to change.** They often stick to "the way things have always been done" and may hesitate to adopt new methods.

- **Confident in their abilities.** Their past successes give them confidence, but they may not see the need to improve further.

- **Risk-averse.** Preferring to stick to tried-and-true methods, they may miss out on innovative opportunities.

- **Reliant on hierarchies.** They often have a top-down approach, with decisions made by senior members and followed by the rest.

Hibernators—Low Team Strength and Fixed Mindset (High End of the Quadrant)

- **Comfort zone dwellers.** Hibernators tend to stick to what they know, even if it's not the most efficient or effective method.

- **Slow to change.** While not entirely resistant to change, they're slow to adopt new methods or strategies.

- **Passive.** They might wait for directions rather than proactively seeking improvements or solutions.

- **Potential for growth.** With the right push or motivation, Hibernators have the potential to move towards a growth mindset.

- **Routine-oriented.** They find comfort in routines and may become uneasy when faced with unfamiliar tasks or situations.

Resisters—Low Team Strength and Fixed Mindset (Bottom End of the Quadrant)

- **Highly resistant to change.** Resisters are set in their ways and often outright reject new ideas or methods.

- **Defensive.** They are quick to defend their methods and resistant to feedback, often seeing it as criticism.

- **Stagnant.** There is minimal growth or progress, as they're content with the status quo, even if it's suboptimal.

- **Pessimistic.** They often focus on limitations and barriers, leading to a negative outlook and reluctance to try new approaches.

- **Isolated**. Collaboration is minimal, and they may prefer working alone, leading to disjointed results and a lack of team cohesion.

How to Move Them to the Vanguard Quadrant
Believers to Vanguards

- **Focus**. Strengthening the team's capabilities while leveraging their already present growth mindset.

- **Skill development**. Invest in training programs to enhance the team's technical and soft skills.

- **Mentorship**. Pair Believers with members from the Vanguard quadrant to learn best practices and effective strategies.

- **Collaborative projects**. Encourage team projects that allow Believers to work closely with Vanguards, absorbing their work ethic and strategies.

- **Feedback loops**. Regularly review their progress, celebrating improvements, and addressing areas of concern.

- **Resource allocation**. Ensure they can access the tools and resources necessary to excel in their roles.

Monoliths to Vanguards

- **Focus**. Shifting the mindset from fixed to growth while maintaining their strong team capabilities.

- **Mindset workshops**. Introduce workshops that challenge their fixed beliefs and showcase the benefits of a growth mindset.

- **Success stories**. Share stories of Vanguards and their achievements to inspire and provide a clear vision.

- **Encourage innovation**. Allow them to lead projects where they can experiment with new strategies, fostering a sense of innovation.

- **Reward adaptability**. Recognize and reward members who showcase adaptability and a willingness to change.

- **Open dialogues**. Create safe spaces for them to voice concerns and fears about change, addressing them constructively.

Hibernators to Vanguards

- **Focus**. Gradual skill enhancement while initiating a shift towards a growth mindset.

- **Incremental challenges**. Introduce them to slightly more challenging tasks over time, gradually pushing them out of their comfort zones.

- **Peer learning**. Encourage learning from peers, especially from Believers with a growth mindset.

- **Positive reinforcement**. Celebrate small victories to build their confidence and showcase the benefits of growth.

- **Skill-based training**. Focus on training that enhances their core skills, making them feel more competent.

- **Mindset shift activities**. Introduce activities that challenge their fixed beliefs, such as brainstorming sessions or problem-solving challenges.

Resisters to Vanguards:

- **Focus**. Addressing resistance to change while slowly building team strength.

- **One-on-one counseling**. Understand their deep-seated fears or reasons for resistance and address them individually.

- **Show tangible benefits**. Showcase the benefits of adopting new methods or mindsets, making the transition worthwhile.

- **Involve in decision making**. Make them feel valued by involving them in decisions, reducing resistance.

- **Small group collaborations**. Pair them with a mix of Believers and Vanguards in small projects, allowing for closer interaction and influence.

- **Continuous feedback**. Regular check-ins to address concerns, provide support, and guide them towards the Vanguard quadrant.

Chapter Tools and Resources

This book contains many valuable tools and resources to help you on the Vanguard journey.

At the end of Chapters 1 to 5, you'll find a quick reference section detailing the tools and resources specific to that chapter (this section for Chapter 1 is located below). These tools, ranging from evaluation frameworks to optimization matrices and workshops, are designed to directly apply the concepts you've learned.

For easy access to these tools, visit our online resource hub at www.vanguardedge.com/resources. You'll find downloadable versions and additional materials to enhance your journey in building a high-performing team.

Embrace these tools as you progress through the book. They are your key to transforming insights into real-world team success.

Chapter 1
Mindset Tools and Resources

Chapter 1 explored the foundational aspect of building a high-performing team: Mindset. To help you assess and develop this critical element, we've introduced two essential tools:

1. Mindset and Strength Evaluation Tool (MSET). This tool is designed to evaluate the prevailing mindsets within your team, identifying areas of strength and opportunities for growth. It's a first step in aligning your team's mindset with the principles of the Vanguard Edge.

2. Vanguard Foundation Framework (VFF). The VFF is a structured approach to building and reinforcing a growth-oriented mindset within your team. It provides a step-by-step guide to cultivating an environment where innovation, adaptability, and continuous learning are at the forefront.

To access these tools and begin the journey of mindset transformation, visit our online resource center at www.vanguardedge.com/resources.

Remember, the right mindset is the bedrock of team success. Utilize these tools to build a strong foundation for your Vanguard team.

Chapter 2

Mission: Charting the Course

....

Good business leaders create a vision, articulate the vision, passionately own the vision, and relentlessly drive it to completion.
—Jack Welch

....

In 2014, Satya Nadella took over as CEO of Microsoft, replacing Steve Ballmer. Microsoft had already fundamentally achieved its original vision—to put a PC on every desk and in every home—and Nadella brought a fresh vision. He pushed his sprawling firm to be more inclusive and forward-looking. He emphasized cloud computing, artificial intelligence, and other emerging technologies.

Moreover, Nadella brought cultural change to the staid Microsoft behemoth. He encouraged his engineers to be innovative, take risks, and learn from their mistakes. He decimated the company's long-standing silos and rewarded those who collaborated across teams. For the first time, Microsoft embraced the open-source community by joining the Linux Foundation and unsealing the .NET framework.

Under Nadella, Microsoft's vision shifted from putting a PC on every desk to "helping everyone in the world perform better." Before long, Microsoft was a different company. It unveiled innovative products, like the Surface tablet and HoloLens. It invested heavily in its cloud platform, diversifying its revenue streams and competing head-to-head with Amazon Web Services.

How did Nadella engineer this transformation? By having a compelling vision and encouraging a growth mindset in his company. Nadella followed the precepts outlined in Chapter 1—coaxing, training, and empowering his teams to move into the Vanguard quadrant. Then, not surprisingly, he followed many of the principles we'll outline in this chapter. He set clear team objectives. He set goals that required his teams to grow and learn new skills, like AI and open-source development. He measured their progress and set milestones for future accomplishments. He *demanded* innovation, risk-taking, and collaboration.

Microsoft's evolution under Nadella is a beautiful example of what happens when a company sets a clear mission, aligns with that mission, structures goals, and balances its long-term vision with short-term objectives. Nadella encouraged open communication, allowing company employees to express their concerns and opinions. He stressed that his teams must be adaptable and capable of pivoting to respond to a fast-changing industry. Throughout the process, he required regular reviews to ensure his teams progressed toward their goals. When they did, he celebrated their achievements. Ultimately, Microsoft and Nadella overcame all the primary challenges facing teams who struggle to define their mission and objectives.

The **GOALS** You Want

I've created the GOALS Model to guide you toward achieving this for your company. GOALS is an acronym that stands for growth-oriented, observable, action-driven, limit-crushing, and shared. For a goal to be effective, it must contain each of these components in any order. Let's break down the parts and talk about why this approach makes sense.

Growth-Oriented

These are goals that promote personal and professional growth. It might be new skills, knowledge, or challenges. For example, you might aim to improve your public speaking, develop new leadership abilities, or master a new coding language.

Observable

This means your goals are based on measurable outcomes or behaviors achieved according to a specific timeline. For instance, you might say you want to "reduce client response time by 30 percent within six months" or "increase productivity by 20 percent in the first quarter." In other words, you set specific, quantifiable indicators of your success that others can see.

Action-Driven

This means your goals are broken down into a series of actionable steps. For instance, one action might be to "attend a professional conference" or "create a weekly progress report." Action-driven means you set clear tasks or milestones along your path to the desired outcome. You don't include every milestone the way a project manager might, but you must include the key ones.

Limit-Crushing

In the GOALS Model, limit-crushing means your goals are a stretch for you or your team. You are pushing the envelope, going outside your comfort zone. What does that mean? It means you might pioneer a new marketing strategy or implement an innovative workflow. For this element of the model, you want to identify key challenges to overcome or opportunities to take risks or innovate.

Shared

This is key. This means your goals must involve collaboration. You cannot have a goal that is only yours. It's a team effort or involves people from other silos and gives them shared responsibility for the outcome. For example, you might say, "improve team communication" or "collaborate on a joint project."

Taking a GOALS approach helps you overcome the challenges we all face in defining our team's mission and objectives. These challenges include the following:

- **Lack of alignment**, where team members have different ideas about the team's purpose. This misalignment leads to confusion and wastes time. To avoid this, involve all team members in the mission-setting process. In particular, engage the Believers. This will ensure buy-in, commitment, and aligned understanding.

- **Vague missions**, which are so broad and nebulous that it's difficult to set action steps or measurable outcomes. Offset this threat by fostering open communication, where people feel free to object, admit confusion, and seek clarification.

- **Outside pressure** from external stakeholders who might try to impose their vision or objectives on the team, clouding the mission's goals. Get around this hurdle by engaging with stakeholders to ensure their expectations align with the team's mission. Limit-crushing isn't comfortable for everyone and you may need to bring people along in order to win together.

- **Changing dynamics**. The GOALS Model allows you to make frequent adjustments as the business landscape shifts. Too often, that mercurial landscape leaves teams uncertain about what to do next. Hold regular check-ins to adjust the mission and objectives in response to the outside business environment. Promote agility and responsiveness. Plan for contingencies. Reward those who bring valuable market intelligence to the group.

- **Fear of commitment**. Yes, this challenge isn't limited to romantic relationships. It happens in business when teams balk at setting limit-crushing goals for fear of failing or concern about the ramifications of missing their objective. The GOALS Model frees you of this concern by encouraging teams to take risks. Remind team members of the value of maintaining a growth mindset.

- **Communication barriers**, which can lead to misunderstandings, confusion, and inefficiency. Diverse teams often have cultural or linguistic differences that impede collaboration. GOALS removes this threat, but it also helps to invest in training sessions focused on good communication and alignment.

Before implementing the GOALS Model, it's imperative that you start with a vision. As the leader, be clear about what you want to achieve. All goals and alignment spill out from a clear mission. During the process, ensure the whole team is helping set specific goals and milestones. This leverages the group's collective intelligence but also ensures commitment. Regular meetings will help reinforce the direction and alignment and motivate team members. Celebrate the little victories along the way and continually provide feedback and encouragement. People perform better when they know someone is paying attention, understanding, and appreciating the work they're doing.

Introducing a new organization concept like GOALS might prompt some team members to roll their eyes. Maybe they've done goal-setting before. But what separates GOALS from processes like SMART goals is its emphasis on growth. It prioritizes personal and professional development. It ensures team members have some immediate, measurable objectives that require them to evolve in their roles and skill sets.

In addition, GOALS adds that element of pushing limits. Most business executives are familiar with author Jim Collin's concept of BHAGs (big, hairy, audacious goals), a hallmark of companies that are built to last. GOALS embraces that idea by encouraging teams to think beyond their limits, fostering innovation and encouraging risk-taking. This is crucial in the breakneck pace of today's business world.

Another advantage is what I call GOALS's "collaborative essence." It requires teamwork and cross-functional agility. Team members bring their skills and their vulnerability to a shared cause, tightly bonding teams and ensuring their success. Likewise, the flexibility built into GOALS reassures team members that modifications are likely, which makes them feel less beholden to the process and more like the designers of the process. What's more, it breaks the vision down into tangible action steps and measurable outcomes. Nothing gives your leaders more pleasure than crossing something off their to-do list; GOALS offers many opportunities to enjoy that pleasure.

Find a more detailed explanation of the GOALS Model with examples for several different industries and job roles on the companion website at www.vanguardedge. com/resources.

Taking Tangible Steps

This is not to say that turning GOALS into action happens on its own. Once your team has used the GOALS Model to set individual goals using the group's collective intelligence, use the Vanguard Vision Roadmap Framework to carve a clear path to achieving those goals together. This framework emphasizes continuous iteration, refinement, and adaptability, and it is a vital part of the overall GOALS process.

VANGUARD VISION ROADMAP

Continuous Iteration, Refinement, Adaptability

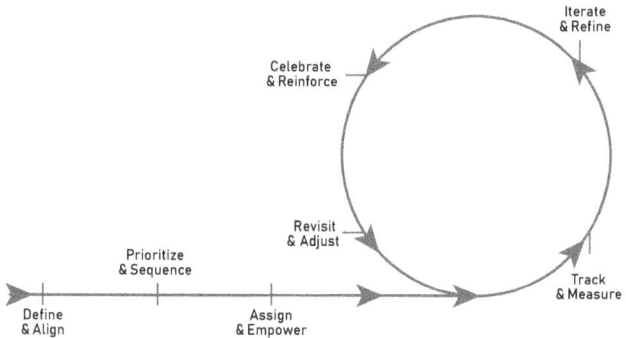

There are seven elements to the framework:

1. **Design and align**. During this first step, you and your team define each goal, and ensure it's aligned with the mission. You start with workshops designed to break the GOALS Model into special action items for the whole team. What is everyone planning to get done?

2. **Prioritize and sequence.** This element ensures you tackle the most crucial goals first by using the Eisenhower Matrix or the MoSCoW Method to prioritize and sequence tasks based on dependencies, urgency, and impact. Find both models on the companion site, with examples.

3. **Assign and empower.** At this stage, you assign roles and responsibilities based on your team members' strengths and skill sets and provide the resources and autonomy each needs to succeed for their own goals and for those they are involved in as part of the team.

4. **Track and measure.** Monitor progress through tracking tools, dashboards, and regular check-ins to ensure accountability.

5. **Iterate and refine.** Using feedback and changing circumstances, you continuously hone your roadmap. At each completed milestone, review your progress, debrief, and adjust as needed.

6. **Celebrate and reinforce.** By acknowledging achievements, you reinforce the mission. So organize celebrations, give shout-outs, and share success stories. Be generous with praise. Don't wait until full completion. Celebrate significant milestones along the way (and maybe a few insignificant ones, too). Proof of success fuels the growth mindset.

7. **Revisit and adjust**. Review the roadmap at least quarterly, ensuring it remains relevant and aligned with your company's goals. Make adjustments based on new data, feedback, or shifts in the organization's direction.

You can easily track this activity using the Vanguard Vision Roadmap (VVR) tracking form, which you can access for free on the companion website (www.vanguardedge. com/resources). Each of the seven elements includes key details that keep you on track.

Staying on Track

Iteration and refinement are the heartbeats of the VVR Framework. Stay agile. Confidently make adjustments. Refining the framework isn't a sign of indecision or faulty foresight. Instead, it reflects your ability to adjust to changing conditions, fresh ideas, and experience. The process is a journey, and as you learn along the way, you gain insights that can help you improve your plan.

One thing that should remain inflexible is the time you devote to recalibration. I recommend quarterly reviews, but don't hesitate to respond when circumstances pose immediate challenges. It also helps to regularly communicate and reinforce your company's broader mission, vision, and values so you can verify that you remain aligned. Remember to use the Vanguard Foundation Framework building blocks we discussed in the last chapter by maintaining trust, clear communication, and a shared vision. Make sure team members understand the value of spotting potential misalignments.

It's easy to drift off course when communication is weak, the overarching mission is hazy, or your organization is growing exponentially. Teams working independently in their own silos can also easily diverge. Avoid these issues with regular audits to see if team goals align with the organizational mission. The key performance indicators you use to ensure progress and accountability can also indicate when you drift off course. When you spot a misalignment, make adjustments and analyze the root cause so you can learn how to avoid it in the future.

Through all this, you and other company leaders must be actively involved, setting goals and maintaining clear communication. There must be a clearly shared, compelling vision. You need to have a stake in the process and show your commitment through empathy and by recognizing the aspirations and challenges team members face. To nurture the right culture, you must be open to feedback and use stories and anecdotes that allow team members to see themselves as part of the overall narrative.

Everything you and other company leaders do and believe spreads throughout the organization. So you need to model the behaviors you want to see. You must be transparent, honest, and reliably keep your promises. You need to delegate and give team members the confidence and autonomy to make decisions (and learn from any mistakes without fear of recrimination). When encountering setbacks, you must embody a growth mindset and stay resilient and optimistic. And other leaders in the company must do the same to create an environment where the team can succeed.

Microsoft's Journey

Before Nadella, Microsoft could have been classified as a Resister or a Hibernator. Its hardware lacked the panache of Apple, and some felt the company was lazily clinging to the one-time dominance of its software platform. It had made a failed foray into smartphones, and its search engine was deep in the shadow of Google. It may not have been floundering, but it was noticeably stuck in the doldrums.

Nadella changed that by setting a clear vision ("mobile-first and cloud-first"). Microsoft prioritized its cloud services and began using its Azure platform to steal business from Amazon. It acquired LinkedIn and GitHub to bolster its enterprise and developer offerings. It created a customer feedback loop, allowing it to respond quickly to challenges. It showed agility by pivoting from the mobile OS market to focus on its cloud and enterprise services. In short, Microsoft created Vanguard teams and followed the principles of the GOALS Model to regain its position as one of the most valued companies in the world.

Key Takeaways

- Microsoft's transformation moved the company from being a potential "Resister" or "Hibernator" to being a Vanguard team. The company shifted from the edge of stagnation to embrace change, innovation, and a growth mindset. It traced the Vanguard Resilience Curve by anticipating changes in the tech industry, quickly adapting, and unifying its response under a new leader. Microsoft adapted its strategies and continued to grow.

- With its shift in focus to cloud computing, open-source development, and strategic acquisitions, Microsoft closely resembled the GOALS Model, ensuring its goals were growth-oriented, observable, action-driven, limit-crushing, and shared. Microsoft defined and aligned its new vision, prioritized its strategies, and assigned roles and responsibilities that were continually tracked, iterated, and celebrated.

- The GOALS Model helps you avoid misalignment, vague missions, outside pressure, changing dynamics, commitment fear, and communication barriers by involving all team members in the mission-setting process, fostering open communication, aligning stakeholder expectations with the team's mission, and planning for contingencies and unexpected changes.

- The Vanguard Vision Roadmap uses seven elements to support continuous iteration and refinement. Goals are aligned, prioritized, assigned, tracked, refined, celebrated, and revisited.

Chapter 2
Mission Tools and Resources

Chapter 2 covers the crucial aspect of defining your team's clear and compelling mission. To assist in this process, we've introduced several tools designed to help you articulate and track your team's mission:

1. GOALS Model. This tool aids in setting clear, achievable goals aligned with your team's mission, ensuring every member understands and works towards these objectives.

2. Vanguard Vision Roadmap Framework (VVR). The VVR helps you create a detailed roadmap for your team's mission, outlining the steps needed to achieve your vision.

3. Eisenhower Matrix and MoSCoW Method. These time-tested methods assist in prioritizing tasks and decisions based on their urgency and importance, aligning daily activities with your overarching mission.

4. Vanguard Vision Roadmap (VVR) Tracking Form. A practical tool to monitor progress along your Vision Roadmap, ensuring your team stays on track and adapts as needed.

Each tool is designed to bring clarity and focus to your team's mission. Access them by visiting our online resource center at www.vanguardedge.com/resources.

Embrace these tools to chart a clear course for your team's success and to keep your mission at the forefront of every action.

Model: Harnessing the Power of Structure and Innovation

....

Organizing is what you do before you do something, so that when you do it, it is not all mixed up
—A.A. Milne

....

LEGO blocks originated in Denmark in the mid-1930s, and in 1949, LEGO introduced its first plastic interlocking brick. The brick was patented in 1958 and proceeded to capture the imaginations of children around the globe, becoming one of the most successful games in marketing history. The company opened theme parks, introduced robotic and customizable bricks, and created light, sound, and pneumatic features for its growing line of toys. In 2000, it was named the "Toy of the Century."

But a few years later, in 2003, LEGO was on the brink of bankruptcy, posting a loss of DKK 1 billion (Danish kroner currency, around $150 million USD). Its profits started declining in 1992, and the company's forays into parks, clothing, figures, and movies diluted its brand and focus further. But the story doesn't end there.

LEGO's leader, Jorgen Vig Knudstorp, reacted by refocusing on its core product and embracing innovation. It reduced its product range by 80 percent, set up cross-functional teams of designers, marketers, and engineers, and launched the LEGO Ideas platform, where fans could submit designs. Fan designs receiving at least ten thousand votes became candidates for commercial production. The process allowed LEGO teams to work collaboratively and take an iterative product development approach. They prototyped quickly, collected feedback, iterated, and released products aligned with customers' needs and wants. By 2015, LEGO was the world's largest toy company by revenue.

The LEGO story underscores the value of creating strong teams that harness each member's strengths and personal preferences. LEGO teams were optimized to move quickly from idea to prototype. The company also serves as a prime example of a company following the principles I described in chapters one and two. They used a growth mindset to reinvent themselves and defined a clear mission. Then LEGO went on to illustrate the importance of creating a management model for a highly functioning team with clear goals, diverse skills and preferences, and measurable milestones along the path of success—the subject of this chapter.

Building the Model

Now that we've fleshed out the importance of mindset and mission in the first two chapters, we can develop the model for your team to operate under. It's not as elaborate as some LEGO designs, but the company exemplified an effective management model. Mindset, mission, and model are intrinsically linked. A team's mindset shapes its beliefs and attitudes, which, in turn, influences its mission or purpose. The mission then provides direction, guiding the team's actions and strategies. The model provides a structural and operational blueprint that ensures a team's mindset and mission effectively translate into actionable strategies and workflows.

When I mention "model," many people automatically picture a traditional org chart, with the CEO occupying the top box and all their direct reports—the chief human resources office, the chief financial officer, the general counsel, and so on.

But those are job titles. The model we want is more about how your team gels and works together, regardless of titles. To build this model, you need to understand and leverage all team members' unique strengths, personalities, and preferences. For example, some leaders prefer clear and precise tasks, while others like open-ended jobs that allow for creativity. Some are visionaries with big ideas, and others are more task-oriented and like executing those big ideas. Some like to address an issue head-on, while others like to think about it and put their thoughts together later in writing.

Each individual is different, but most companies never map their team members' strengths and weaknesses in a logical or methodical way. They are missing something important as a result. They are missing the opportunity to bring together a diversity of perspectives, skills, and experiences in a way that leads to comprehensive solutions. Teams that brainstorm together, trust each other, and feel free to be vulnerable or direct are better able to share their ideas. This helps them find better solutions and surface more innovative ideas, which is far better than a compromise or a simplistic idea everyone lazily accepts because they all think the same way or are not confident enough to speak up.

The Vanguard Team Optimization Framework (VTOF) and the companion Vanguard Team Optimization Matrix (VTOM) are instrumental in this process. The VTOF tells you what to collect and the VTOM is the tool you use to store the information you collected. Just as LEGO leader Jørgen Vig Knudstorp aligned team strengths with business objectives, you can use VTOF and VTOM to gather data on each team member's strengths, preferences, and interaction style to tailor workflows effectively. By dedicating time each month for teams to brainstorm, collaborate on solutions, and share diverse ideas, leaders create a structured space for innovation.

The innovation that emerges from a diverse team is hugely advantageous to your company. To help groups get there, I developed the Vanguard Creativity and Innovation Session (VCIS). This monthly program brings diverse groups together and helps them think, create, innovate, and collaboratively solve problems. The VCIS also allows leaders to demonstrate that failure is allowed, even valued, when teams learn and grow from the experience. It helps teams from retreating to their silos, where everybody does their own thing.

**VANGUARD CREATIVITY
& INNOVATION MODEL**

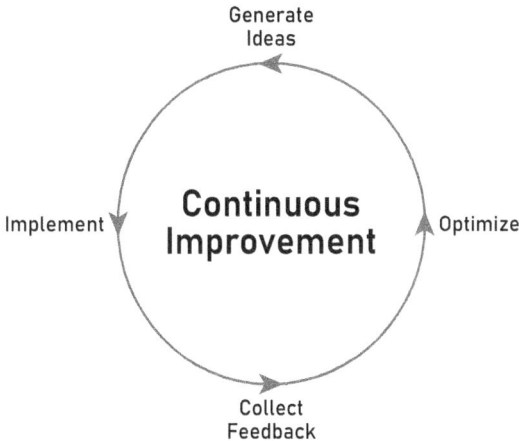

Generate
Ideas

Implement

**Continuous
Improvement**

Optimize

Collect
Feedback

Inside the VCIS

The Vanguard Creativity and Innovation Session (VCIS) promotes innovation in a simple, straightforward, monthly activity that easily integrates with any team's size, routine, or industry.

A vital element of the session is hearing external perspectives by periodically inviting an industry expert or thought leader to meet the team. Another option is to bring in members of other teams for a different perspective. You can also have collaborative sessions with business partners, suppliers, or key clients.

Once or twice a year, hold an "Open VCIS" session where anyone from the organization can come and share ideas, regardless of the department or role. You can also expand it by inviting loyal customers. It's also helpful to set up an email address or online portal where people outside the core team can submit ideas or ask the team questions. Many successful teams also have an occasional workshop, inviting cross-functional partners or teams and using a facilitator to ensure strong participation. Use brief surveys to gather feedback from team members and outside participants. It's also a good idea to acknowledge and even reward significant contributions from those outside the core team.

This is a crucial point: Even Vanguard teams can atrophy and return to one of the other quadrants if the leader isn't purposeful, and if the team doesn't actively work to prevent that from happening. The same is true about your mission and your model—it takes hard work and regular reminders of what your mindset, mission, and model really are. If you don't reiterate these three Ms often, teams will fall back to whatever their default was. This is what happened to Microsoft. It happened to LEGO. Whatever you put in place, you have to work to maintain it.

Strengths Assessments

There are a number of tools out there to assess the strengths of your team—Myers-Briggs, Gallup StrengthsFinder, and the Kolbe-A are all great assessments. We recommend all three as part of the Vanguard journey. We also provide an assessment with our program—the Vanguard Team Interaction Preference (VTIP) assessment. All four assessments are easily located on the companion website (www.vanguardedge.com/resources), and the VTIP is included at no additional charge. The VTIP measures how people like to communicate, collaborate, and contribute to a team. Coupling the VTIP results with the other assessments gives you a good picture of the team's strengths and opportunities. You can plug the results into a matrix and make good decisions about what each person's team role will be—regardless of the job title. Leaders can assign roles and responsibilities that align with individual strengths.

How It Works: The Vanguard Team Optimization Framework

The VTOF assesses and enhances the interpersonal dynamics of a Vanguard team. A leader starts by tracking team members' strengths, preferences, and potential friction points using the Vanguard Team Optimization Matrix.

The VTOF first includes individual profiles, instinctive problem-solving modes, strengths and talents, and interaction preferences. The profiles include personality traits gleaned from the Myers-Briggs Type Indicator, problem-solving from the Kolbe-A Index, strengths from CliftonStrengths, and interaction preferences from the Vanguard Team Interaction Preference Assessment (VTIP). This data is all included in the matrix (VTOM), which we'll explain in just a bit.

With the individual profiles fleshed out, the leader does a team synergy analysis by aggregating the team's collective strengths, pinpointing potential friction areas (such as communication styles, work ethic and commitment, and cultural or background differences), proposing mitigation strategies, and identifying the team's collaboration strengths and enhancement areas. The third component, feedback mechanisms, involves facilitating team members to share feedback on their peers' collaborative and communication styles and reflect on their own roles and interactions. From these three elements, actionable strategies and recommendations emerge, including these:

- Optimal team structuring, including potential modifications in team composition to enhance dynamics

- Tailored communication protocols, including bespoke strategies designed for the team's unique character

- Collaboration boosters, or tools and practices that amplify team collaboration

Implementing the framework is a seven-step process:

1. Distribute assessments, reassuring participants that it is confidential.

2. Collect and collate data from the individual profiles and feedback mechanisms.

3. Analyze the data to discern patterns, strengths, and areas for enhancement.

4. Encapsulate the team's dynamics in a detailed report (VTOM), complemented with actionable insights.

5. Discuss the findings collaboratively with the team.

6. Craft an action plan based on the VTOM's insights.

7. Periodically reassess the VTOM, particularly when the team shifts significantly.

The VTOF boosts team unity and team members' appreciation for and understanding of each other. It also gives leaders actionable strategies that help them elevate the team's work. The team develops a culture of continuous growth and introspection and learns how to proactively address potential conflicts so it can enjoy smoother operations.

Designing a Vanguard Team Optimization Matrix (VTOM)

The framework's companion document is the VTOM, which is typically a spreadsheet with twelve headers:

- Column A: Team Member Names

- Column B: MBTI Profile

- C: Kolbe-A Index Result

- D: Top 5 Strengths (such as Clifton Strengths)

- E: VTIP Category

- F: Overall VTIP Score

- G: Patterns & Commonalities

- H: Potential Conflicts

- I: Complementary Strengths

- J: Assigned Role

- K: Sub-Team/Project Group

- L: Communication & Collaboration Strategy

After filling in the team's members and their results in columns B–F, use columns G, H, and I to note patterns, highlight potential conflicts, and list complementary strengths and problem-solving modes.

From there, use the data to assign roles, noting them in Column J. Add any sub-teams to column K. Finally, develop (see sidebar on Tailor Communication Guidelines) and note those in column L.

Examples of Tailored Communication Guidelines

- For urgent matters, use phone calls or instant messaging. For less time-sensitive topics, emails or team collaboration platforms are preferred.

- During virtual meetings, keep your camera on to foster engagement. If you need to step away or face interruptions, use the chat function to inform the team.

- For emails, aim to respond within twenty-four hours on weekdays. For instant messages during work hours, try to reply within two hours.

- When sharing updates or news with the team, use bullet points for clarity. Attach relevant documents and highlight key takeaways.

- On a separate sheet or section, periodically record team member feedback. You can use another sheet to record training sessions, workshops, and resources offered to team members. Some leaders use color coding, data validation dropdowns, filters, graphics, and comments to add nuance and depth to their document.

Vanguard Team Interaction Preference Assessment (VTIP)

This assessment helps reveal each team member's interaction style. It's a tool for facilitating better communication, collaboration, and overall team synergy. It covers three topics—team dynamics, collaboration styles, and communication preferences—and includes thirty prompts, each with three options for answering.

Communication Preferences

- 10–15 points: Direct, open communicator who prefers immediate, face-to-face interactions

- 16–25 points: Reflective, structured communicator adaptable to both immediate and planned communications

- 26–30 points: Prefers to reflect and communicate through structured media; values written communication and structured feedback

Collaboration Styles

- 10–15 points: Proactive and leadership-oriented; prefers to lead discussions and projects

- 16–25 points: Supportive and resourceful; can lead or follow, depending on the situation

- 26–30 points: Analytical and driven by feedback; prefers to analyze, seek external expertise, and work collaboratively

Team Dynamics

- 10–15 points: Visionary and proactive in team settings; often takes the lead and is energized by leading or presenting

- 16–25 points: Collaborative and consensus-driven; actively participates in discussions and values a balanced team approach

- 26–30 points: Reflective and goal-oriented; observes, absorbs information, and ensures alignment with broader goals

Participants will receive a score for each category between 10 and 30 points. Then they'll also receive a total score, ranging from 30 to 90. The total score will assign participants to a distinct role that reflects their preferences, based on their answers. Here's what that looks like:

1. **30–45 points: The Initiator**. This person is direct, proactive, and leadership-oriented. Prefers immediate communication and often takes the lead in discussions and projects. Energized by leading or presenting. This action-oriented team member often jumps into tasks headfirst, making them great for getting projects off the ground and driving momentum.

2. **46–60 points: The Collaborator**. Balanced and adaptable, a collaborator can lead or follow, depending on the situation, and actively participates in discussions. This resourceful person values a team approach and can wear many hats. They're excellent at bridging gaps between team members and can adapt to various roles as needed.

3. **61–75 points: The Strategist**. The strategist is reflective, analytical, and goal-oriented. Prefers structured communication and is driven by analysis and feedback. Ensures alignment with broader goals and often seeks external expertise. The strategist is a planner and thinker who ensures the team aligns with broader objectives and provides a deeper analysis of challenges.

4. **76–90 points: The Harmonizer.** A deep thinker, the harmonizer values written communication and structured feedback. A great observer who absorbs information and ensures team cohesion and harmony by happily working collaboratively. They ensure everyone is on the same page and that the team environment is positive and productive. The glue that holds the team together.

Assembling a Team

The most effective teams are balanced, ensuring the team can initiate, plan, execute, and harmonize effectively. Here's an example composition of an optimal, seven-member team:

- **Two initiators** will drive the team forward with momentum and action. They will kick off discussions and projects and help set the pace and direction.

- **Two collaborators** will bridge the gap between initiators and strategists and ensure ideas become action items. They are versatile and adapt to various roles, although you count on them to mediate discussions and ensure all voices are heard.

- **Two strategists** provide the analytical and planning power to the team. They'll ensure team actions align with broader objectives and provide deeper insights into challenges. Their reflective nature will be crucial in making informed decisions.

- **One harmonizer,** particularly a strong one, ensures cohesion, a positive environment, and conflict resolution. Harmonizers ensure everyone is aligned and feels valued.

Vanguard Creativity and Innovation Session (VCIS)

This monthly brainstorming session fosters a culture of creativity and innovation. The team welcomes all ideas and strives to build on those ideas. The goal is to find an idea they can act on within a month or set the stage for a future rollout. Here's how these sessions are structured:

- **Week 1: Idea submission**
  - Team members jot down innovative ideas or improvements they've thought of throughout the month.
  - Ideas can be submitted anonymously or with names attached based on team preference.

- **Week 2: Collaborative brainstorming**
  - Team members discuss the submitted ideas for an hour, aiming to refine and combine ideas (but not critique them).

- **Week 3: Idea selection**
  - The team votes on one idea (or a combination of ideas) to focus on for the next month. Voting can be a show of hands or an online poll.

- **Week 4: Implementation and review**
  - The team dedicates time to implement the idea or plan its rollout.

     ○   At the end of the month, the team reviews the impact or progress of the idea.

VCIS ensures creativity and innovation are recurring themes for the team. It helps team members bond, learn, and collaborate. The team can see real results to celebrate by focusing on actionable ideas.

Teams can also invite outside experts to their VCIS. These experts can come from another company, a different industry, or from another team within their company. They can also invite business partners, suppliers, or key clients for collaborations. Once or twice a year, the team can hold an "Open VCIS" that anyone from the organization can attend to share ideas. The team can even invite members of the public.

Teams should also set up feedback channels, such as an email address or an online portal, where people not on the team can submit ideas. Some team meetings can also be transformed into a workshop where cross-functional teams, partners, or other stakeholders come in to collaborate. Always share a brief survey with internal and external participants to help the team improve. Teams can encourage participation by recognizing significant contributions or implementing an outside idea.

Ad Hoc Teams

When opportunities pop up—as they often do for companies with a growth mindset—you can create a custom-designed, ad hoc, small team to work on it. You don't need the whole team working on it, and the small group includes team members who fit together well.

This is not to say the ad hoc team will work seamlessly together. If well composed, they are a diverse group, with different backgrounds and attitudes. So you're bound to have some conflicts even in a handpicked group. The goal, however, is not to mediate these differences for a less-than-optimal compromise. Instead, you want to *navigate* these conflicts to reach the best solution. Team members whose viewpoints aren't incorporated into a solution—the hallmark of a compromise—must understand that their alternative viewpoints were vital to driving the team to the best solution.

These helpful attitudes emerge from the month-long innovation sessions we discussed in the last section of this chapter. These sessions are crucial. They provide some rhythm that coaxes people to think innovatively every day and allow all types of people to bring forth their ideas. For example, I'm one of those people who is happy blurting out ideas as they occur to me. But others like to think through their ideas privately and bring forth well-thought-out ideas. If you don't have the continuity and depth of the innovation sessions, these people often get left out because they can't formulate their ideas on the spot. And even if they can, they may need time to let them simmer.

The innovation session fosters this approach. You dedicate time each month for teams to brainstorm and share ideas—sometimes informally through emails or lunchroom chats—and it all culminates in the fourth week of the session when all the great ideas are brought to the table. Then you can implement the best ideas right away.

This approach is quite different from the typical process where a discussion begins the process. Then the team continually refines it for three or four weeks. With that approach, many great ideas die on the vine or never make it to the table.

But, like I said, it all starts with the optimization framework. The framework guides how you collect information about your team members; the matrix is where you store that data. The Creativity and Innovation session is a second framework that governs internal ideation. The team leader is the ultimate arbiter of the team's work, but the matrix is available to everyone. When team members start to interact, they already have an idea of what to expect regarding the behavior and attitudes of their colleagues.

Understanding Failure

A vital piece of this process is for you to recognize people for appropriate risk-taking. No one likes to fail, of course, but failures are springboards to solutions on a Vanguard team with a growth mindset. They aren't bad. They are learning experiences. Remember, Vanguard teams are not on the traditional resilience curve, where workers fear losing their jobs or point fingers when something doesn't work as planned. Vanguard team members subscribe to Thomas Edison's attitude, embodied in this quote: "I didn't fail ten thousand times to develop a light bulb. I learned ten thousand ways that don't work."

Let me make a critical distinction here: These teams aren't celebrating failure. They are celebrating the insights that result from failure and risk-taking. And as we've said before, behavior that gets rewarded gets repeated. If you take risks, learn, and earn praise for advancing the cause, you become even more eager to find the answer, taking whatever risks that help you along the way.

Again, take LEGO as an example: Before they made their big turnaround, the company was involved in a wide variety of ventures. It got into movies. It built a theme park. It brought out action figures that weren't really LEGOs. They had run so far afield from their original mission—to provide building blocks for inventive people to explore their imaginations—that they had lost their way. They had no clear path to make money anymore. They were failing in a way they couldn't celebrate. They weren't learning from the failures and risk-taking.

So the company's leaders asked themselves, "How can we get back to the basics? We don't want to close LEGOLAND or quit making LEGO movies, but how do we return the focus to our core product and innovate from there?" That's when they developed their Star Wars and Indiana Jones products and made an Eiffel Tower–scale model that was the tallest LEGO set you could buy. In time, they were able to return to the core product and mission with a host of innovative ideas.

Potential Obstacles When Shaping Team Models and Cultures

Change fatigue is a real thing. Change, particularly constant change, wears people out. When people experience change fatigue, they resist *any* type of change, even change for the better. All they see is change, and they can get pretty tired of it.

The answer to this problem is to let people be heard. Be mindful that people have different tolerance levels for change, and some won't accommodate it as easily as others. It's crucial that you let team members voice their concerns about change. If you ask them for their help in designing the change—if you communicate the need and involve them in the process—they not only won't resist; they'll also embrace the change.

If you don't give people a chance to have a say, then whatever is handed down will feel ill-informed to them. And if they view the decision as ill-informed, they won't adopt it. They don't see it as a rational decision because they didn't have a say. Here's an easy way to remember that: When change happens *to* people, they resist it. When change happens *with* people, they embrace it.

The matrix of individual preferences helps you navigate this. If you know who likes to communicate face-to-face immediately and those who prefer to communicate via email after a period of time, you're in a better position to manage change. You're better able to mediate misunderstandings because you can spot the source of those conflicts. As a neutral third party, you can mediate and moderate team disputes productively.

Transitioning to a Vanguard model is done in phases. It's not done overnight. You start by introducing the concepts to everyone on the team. Then you conduct assessments, such as the VTIP, to understand team dynamics. Then you use tools like the VTOM to visualize and analyze team data. Then it becomes a process of iteration and review based on team feedback. Throughout the process—as you attend the creativity and innovation sessions and watch people interact—you develop clear data points that you can plug into your matrix. This allows you to make the best-informed decisions about the team and for the team to decide the issues themselves.

We'll talk about metrics in the next chapter, but for now, understand that clear performance indicators are crucial. People need to know their mission and goals and how their progress will be measured. And they need check-ins, feedback sessions, and reassessments to let them know how they're doing.

All of our tools, models, and frameworks work perfectly well with virtual teams, too. It helps to have rules for virtual team interaction to ensure people are present in the moment and not multitasking. Another benefit is how easily the tools, frameworks, and models can be customized. For example, a sales team might want to add a selling assessment to the VTOM. These are frameworks—suggestions of how we've seen it done successfully. Feel free to experiment with what works best for you.

The Vanguard Model is also adaptable to transitions, such as when a new team member or leader joins the company when the market shifts, or when other external factors prompt changes, such as when BlackBerry moved from one product to a different industry. The Vanguard model is strong enough to withstand these curveballs. Your team doesn't have to disband when a new CEO takes the helm.

Key Takeaways

- Once you've developed individual profiles of each team member's personality traits, instinctive problem-solving modes, strengths and talents, and interaction preferences, you can conduct a team synergy analysis. You aggregate the team's strengths, pinpoint potential friction areas, propose mitigation strategies (conflict forecasting), and identify the team's collaboration strengths and enhancement needs. Be sure to build in feedback mechanisms, such as encouraging team members to talk about their teammates' collaborative and communication styles while also reflecting on their own roles and interactions. With that data, you can suggest team modifications, tailored communication approaches, and additional tools and practices to amplify the team's collaboration.

- LEGO's return to prominence as a toymaker underscores the value of team synergy. LEGO built cross-functional teams to harness the company's diverse perspectives and skill sets and fostered a culture of innovation and creativity through quick prototyping, feedback collection, and iteration. Its LEGO Ideas platform harnessed the creativity of its loyal customers and allowed continuous innovation as the company paired external creativity with its internal expertise.

• LEGO's rejuvenation reflects the model we describe in this chapter. That model emphasizes building stronger teams through carefully assessing personality traits, work and communication preferences, continual feedback, and iteration to improve the team and heighten its results. Using this modeling approach, your action plans find better traction, and you build flexible, resilient teams that can adjust to internal and external changes.

• LEGO also reinforced the principles we discussed in Chapters 1 ("Mindset") and 2 ("Mission"). LEGO CEO Jørgen Vig Knudstorp saw LEGO's challenges as an opportunity for innovation and transformation, demonstrating a growth mindset that filtered throughout his company. Moreover, he led his company through a redefinition of its mission, resurrecting its core values and strengths by focusing on the iconic LEGO brick and streamlining its product range.

Chapter 3
Model Tools and Resources

Chapter 3 focuses on your team's model, emphasizing the importance of structure and innovation. To facilitate this, we introduce tools that help in optimizing your team's operational framework:

1. Vanguard Team Optimization Framework (VTOF). *The VTOF guides you in structuring your team for maximum efficiency and effectiveness, ensuring that each member's role and responsibilities are clearly defined and aligned with team goals.*

2. Vanguard Team Optimization Matrix (VTOM). *The VTOM assists in assessing and mapping out the strengths and areas for development within your team, allowing for targeted improvements and strategic alignment.*

3. Vanguard Creativity and Innovation Session (VCIS). *This tool fosters creativity and innovation within your team, encouraging new ideas and approaches that can be integrated into your operational model.*

4. Vanguard Team Interaction Preference Assessment (VTIP). *The VTIP helps understand your team members' preferred communication and interaction styles, enhancing collaboration and efficiency.*

These tools are vital in building a robust and innovative team structure. To access them, visit our online resource center at www.vanguardedge.com/resources.

Leverage these tools to create a team structure that is efficient, adaptable, and conducive to innovation.

Chapter 4

Message: Creating a Team Voice That Resonates

The single biggest problem in communication is the illusion that it has taken place.
—George Bernard Shaw

Pixar burst on the scene in 1995 with *Toy Story*, the first fully computer-animated feature film. In the years since, Pixar has released twenty-seven movies and earned more than $15 billion worldwide, an average of more than $500 million per film.

What set Pixar apart—and what prompted Disney to pay over $7 billion for it in 2006—was the Pixar "Braintrust" team. The Braintrust team—its actual name—is the internal and external engine that runs Pixar's design team and ensures that all its films embody the studio's unique and engaging messaging.

Disney chief Bob Iger made it clear that Disney was investing in that Braintrust. He bought Pixar because it produces excellent animated films, but that was just one reason. The other reason was the value he saw in Pixar's discipline about its message. Although Pixar would remain largely independent, Iger felt Pixar's messaging approach to filmmaking would revitalize Disney's own almost-century-old animation studio. Pixar's Braintrust team was so good that its team brand was bigger than the company itself and valuable enough to compel Disney to buy it.

That is the power of a strong team and a strong team brand. And the story of that Pixar team is an ideal way to underscore the value of messaging when you are a Vanguard team.

As we've noted already, each chapter in this book builds on the previous chapter. First, we identify and develop a growth mindset, and then we develop a mission for your team. In the last chapter, we talked about how to model that team.

This chapter focuses on basic messaging—in other words, how to tell the story. Many teams struggle with this vital work. The team's mission may be clear to team members, but it also has to be articulated in a clear and compelling way to internal and external stakeholders, including the media, stockholders, and communities where the company conducts business.

It's also important to note that while teams of all levels in an organization can become Vanguard teams, this M is nuanced depending on your team's level in the organization. For example, the CEO can shape messaging for the whole company while also working on the executive team. A director will need to make sure that their team's messaging aligns with the company's overall messaging. Much of this chapter will focus on executive-level messaging. Still, you can easily use many of these messaging components by separating them from the tools that don't fit your team's role in the company.

By crafting a clear, compelling message, teams can rally support, secure resources, and drive change within and outside the organization.

To help you accomplish this, I recommend three tools:

- **The Vanguard Message Blueprint**, a way of building your messaging framework. The blueprint is your North Star; it guides all your communications and includes a core message.

- **The Vanguard Message Playbook**, which ensures all your messengers—whether a small internal team or a larger contingent from your marketing team to your IT, project, and product leaders—deliver a message that matches the Vanguard team's message. The playbook also helps you train new employees or team members.

- **The Vanguard Voice Workshop**, a quarterly session that reviews the message and ensures everyone is aligned. The workshop is also an opportunity for stakeholders to help craft or refine messages and storyboards for new products, services, or projects, ensuring messages are consistent.

VANGUARD MESSAGE BLUEPRINT

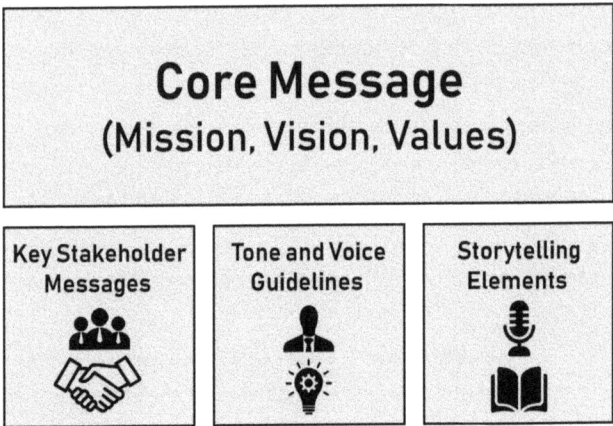

Core Message
(Mission, Vision, Values)

| Key Stakeholder Messages | Tone and Voice Guidelines | Storytelling Elements |

Key Elements of a Strong Message

The core message from any team would articulate the team's purpose, what it stands for, and its vision. It should also have tone and voice guidelines. What kind of words does the message use? How do those words resonate? Should the message be delivered in a playful, irreverent way, or should it be lofty, visionary? What storytelling elements should we use to ensure our story resonates— that it's relatable and memorable?

Successful teams carve out a distinct personal niche that harmonizes with the company's overarching identity. A powerful team message transcends mere words with a vivid picture of the team's mission, vision, and values, all expressed in a voice that resonates deeply. It's about the emotional undertones, the stories that breathe life into the message, and the authenticity that makes it believable.

Having a unified team voice ensures a consistent message, thought, and brand. It signals reliability. When your message is compelling and consistent time after time, people view it as professional. They believe you're competent. They know what to expect from you, and this makes you more trustworthy. In short, it helps you build stronger relationships with both external and internal stakeholders, and it can drive more meaningful interactions with them.

Pixar's core message is that humanity does not end with humans. It's in toys, cars, and monsters, too. Experts from business to psychology have weighed in over the years on what Pixar films truly represent. According to *Discover* magazine, Pixar's twenty-seven films "affect how we define the rights of millions, perhaps billions, in the coming century." Rats will cook. Houses will fly. Monsters will care. Machines will love. In fact, love conquers all, Mr. Potato Head.

The feedback you get—such as through the Vanguard Voice Workshop—is crucial to refining and iterating your core narrative. You should welcome internal and external feedback. Surveys are an excellent tool, but you can also learn a lot from market trends. Regular team check-ins help you stay on track, as do check-ins with other departments you interact with. Many goals are cross-departmental, so your colleagues' feedback is critical.

For Pixar, feedback comes most strikingly through the box office. A good example is *Lightyear*, the studio's spinoff from its *Toy Story* franchise. The three *Toy Story* films did incredibly well, but *Lightyear*, which takes the Buzz Lightyear character out of the *Toy Story* narrative, failed miserably. You can bet that the Pixar Braintrust will adjust and learn from *Lightyear*'s difficulties. The public gave them feedback with their dollars.

How to Craft a Great Message

The Vanguard Message Blueprint is basically your team's North Star; it guides all your communications and includes your core message.

Your communications need to include that core message, but you should still tailor what you say to different audiences. You don't speak to your staff the same way you speak to your stockholders or customers. Your blueprint should outline your communication style, words, and branding guidelines. It includes messaging phrases and describes the tone of voice you strive for, be it conversation or technical, serious or lighthearted. It should also include sample messages for each stakeholder so that people who need to write a message have a rubric to consult.

The Vanguard Message Playbook takes it a step further, describing what communication channels to use and how often to use them. For employees, for example, you may use email, an internal SharePoint site, or the company newsletter. For the public, you might use certain social media platforms with a prescribed regularity. Your playbook should also include a calendar to track and signal key communication opportunities, such as an investor call or an annual report, and provide templates and scripts designed for specific audiences. It should also describe the feedback loop. How do you measure the effectiveness of your communications? How do you accept and respond to stakeholder feedback? Which questions from stakeholders should be elevated to a place in the FAQ section of your website?

The playbook empowers team members to embody, champion, and amplify the message, ensuring that every voice strengthens the collective chorus.

The playbook should also include a crisis communication plan. Having thought about potential crises ahead of time will make your decisions easier to make in the moment. Pixar, again, is a good example. When *Lightyear* came out in 2020, many criticized it as being "too woke" because of a brief scene in which two same-sex characters share a kiss. Should Pixar or Disney weigh in on the question and explain their reasons for the scene?

They chose not to, but that doesn't mean the studio didn't anticipate the controversy. In fact, Disney had considered cutting the scene until LBGTQ+ employees objected. In the end, neither Disney nor Pixar engaged in the debate, letting their film speak for itself.

The final step in crafting a great message involves the Vanguard Voice Workshop, where team members dive deeply into the blueprint and playbook. They practice storyboarding project campaigns that reflect the core message. They practice answering questions with the media, receiving real-time feedback that ensures they stay on point.

Ensuring Message Clarity and Consistency

Failing to be steady and reliable with your messaging can dilute your brand and hurt your business. Again, look at Pixar. If they had five different teams developing movies, each would be different, guided by different ideas and values. But people have come to rely on Pixar to tell great, uplifting stories that tickle our imaginations and allow us to see the wonder in our world.

The key to ensuring team members deliver consistent messaging that aligns with your organization's broader narrative starts with the Vanguard Voice Workshop (see the How to Craft a Great Message sidebar). Not every employee will be able to attend a workshop—it's for key internal stakeholders—but they can have access to the blueprint and playbook. These provide leaders with the tools they need to brief the entire company regularly. Done right, even the lowest or newest employees should be able to say, "This is who we are. This is what we stand for. This is our message."

Just as you must periodically recalibrate your team model and matrix when you get a new team member or leader, you must continue to refine your blueprint and playbook as conditions change. It's not a "one and done." These are iterative, evergreen documents. They work in tandem, so when you update the blueprint, you also must update the playbook and then train or communicate the changes to your company.

When the team narrative needs to change, navigate the challenge through the following:

- **Transparency**. Leaders should clearly explain the reasons for the change and ensure the team understands the rationale.

- **Inclusive decision-making**. Seek team members' input and feedback.

- **Utilize tools**. Update your blueprint and playbook, and offer training to ensure team members are aligned with the new message.

I can't say enough about how important clear and consistent messaging is. I see examples all the time of companies that crow about their core values. They print their values in the annual report. They etch them into their email signatures. They paint their core values on the wall in their lobby. But when you start to work with that company, you quickly find that they don't embody their core values *at all*. They say they value employees, their most important assets. But then they announce a massive, indiscriminate, and unapologetic layoff. There's a tremendous gap between what they say and how they act, and it completely breaks any trust they had with their stakeholders. They stop believing what the company says. It hurts your recruitment, and it hurts your retention.

Balancing Team Identity with the Larger Company

When you develop a distinct team identity, and you consistently message that out to everyone else, you also have to communicate why people should care. What's in it for them? The parent company has the same challenge. They must communicate how others benefit from the work they are doing.

So it pays to be clear: "When we do our work, this is how you benefit." You avoid conflicting with the organization's broader strategy by focusing on how you contribute to it and provide benefits to boot. You're aligned, yet unique. Remember, a Vanguard team does not live in a closed system. It's part of a feedback loop and needs that feedback to avoid atrophy and improve. Being in tune with the greater mission is vital to that. Your team system may be running smoothly, but you must adjust if it's not producing the necessary results because it's out of step with the company. You need the feedback that alerts you to that.

If you do everything right—adopt the right mindset, set a clear mission and team model, and follow consistent, clear messaging—you will build a strong internal team brand. None of this takes care of itself. It requires ongoing work, reflection, tweaking, and communication. If you utilize all the tools we've talked about in the first three chapters and celebrate your successes—including the modest ones—your small wins turn into big wins.

Teams can celebrate and showcase their success through dedicated communication channels, such as blogs or newsletters, by hosting team events to highlight achievements and stories and by engaging in Vanguard Voice Workshops. Celebrating these moments fuels morale and fortifies the team's sub-brand. These celebrations recognize that while the team is part of a larger construct, it has its own vibrant identity.

In addition, make sure stakeholders understand how *they* benefit from your successes. They need to know that your success is their success—that your team's success is success for the company. A great team might evoke a little envy or jealousy. That's okay. There is nothing wrong with people thinking, *I want to work for that team* or *I want my name associated with them*.

We also included some sample Vanguard Message Blueprints, Playbooks, and Workshop agendas on the companion website for different team levels in the sample organizations (www.vanguardedge.com/resources).

Key Takeaways

- Many teams struggle with basic messaging and storytelling. The team's mission may be clear to team members, but it must be articulated to internal and external stakeholders as well. A clear, compelling message can help you rally support, secure resources, and drive change.

- A team's core message should articulate the team's purpose, what it stands for, and its vision. The team should also have tone and voice guidelines. Team members should ask themselves, "What storytelling elements should we use to ensure our story resonates—that it's relatable and memorable?"

- A unified team signals reliability. When your message is compelling and consistent time after time, people view it as professional. They believe you're competent. They know what to expect from you, and this makes you more trustworthy.

- Feedback is crucial to refining your core narrative. Surveys are an excellent tool, but you can learn a lot from market trends, team check-ins, and check-ins with other departments. Your colleagues' feedback is critical.

- Tailor your core message to different audiences. Address stockholders or customers differently than you would employees. Include messaging phrases and tone-of-voice descriptions in your Vanguard Message Blueprint. Your Vanguard Message Playbook should describe what communication channels to use and how often to use them.

- Inconsistent messaging can dilute your brand and hurt your business. That said, recalibrate your blueprint and playbook as conditions change. These are iterative, evergreen documents that work in tandem, so when you update the blueprint, update the playbook accordingly and then train or communicate the changes to your company.

- Communicate why people should care. Be clear: "When we do our work, this is how you benefit." Avoid conflicting with the organization's broader strategy by focusing on how you contribute to that larger effort and add benefit, too. Feedback helps your team avoid atrophy and improve.

Chapter 4
Message Tools and Resources

Chapter 4 is dedicated to messaging, focusing on creating and communicating a team voice that genuinely resonates. To assist in this vital aspect of team dynamics, we introduce several tools designed to refine and amplify your team's message:

1. Vanguard Message Blueprint. This tool helps you construct a clear, impactful message that encapsulates your team's mission, values, and goals. It's a guide to creating a narrative that resonates within and outside your team.

2. Vanguard Message Playbook. The playbook offers strategies and techniques for consistently communicating your team's message across various platforms and interactions, ensuring coherence and clarity in all communications.

3. Vanguard Voice Workshop. This interactive workshop is designed to engage your team members in developing a unified voice, fostering a deeper understanding and commitment to the team's core message.

These tools are essential for crafting a message that communicates your team's purpose and inspires *action and commitment. To access these resources, visit our online resource center at www.vanguardedge. com/resources.*

Utilize these tools to ensure your team's message is heard, felt, and acted upon.

Chapter 5

Metrics: Quantifying Team Success

*Measure what is measurable, and make
measurable what is not so.*
—Galileo Galilei

In 2015, the Leicester City soccer team in England was in a precarious position. After a miserable season in the English Premier League, it was on the brink of relegation. The prospect of a demotion left the vibrant city in a somber mood, and many players worried about their careers. The team needed nothing short of a miracle.

That miracle arrived in the form of a pizza-loving Italian manager who had never won a championship. Claudio Ranieri arrived in Leicester with a sense of purpose, which he quickly instilled in his players. Unlike many coaches, who shape their teams into a preconceived unit based on the coach's vision, Ranieri instead shaped his team according to his players' strengths. He doubled down on the blistering pace of his best players, including midfielder Riyad Mahrez and striker Jamie Vardy, and the unbending defense of Wes Morgan.

Moreover, the team began tracking key performance metrics for each player. These key performance indicators

(KPIs) went well beyond wins and losses, minutes played, goals scored, and goals allowed. Instead, the team tracked players' fitness levels, passing success, possession time, and goal conversion rates. The team measured any aspect of the players' games that might contribute to the team's success, and each player could see clearly where they were improving and what areas they needed to work on. Each player was given a role and the tools to excel in that role. They embodied a Vanguard Continuous Improvement Framework (VCIF) and sent the message that though underdogs, they would fight with every ounce of skill and energy they possessed.

The result was that Leicester started to win. A lot. In the second year of Ranieri's stint, the team beat the 5,000-to-1 odds to become Premier League champions. The city erupted in joy, and the team went on to play admirably in the UEFA Champions League. Vardy and Mahrez became household names. Ranieri was hailed as a genius.

Sports always make great metaphors, and in all the important ways, Leicester was a model of the Vanguard team. Like a Vanguard team leader, Ranieri carefully assessed his players' strengths, plugged them into a matrix, and found a lineup that allowed each player's unique abilities to shine. The team's mission was clear, and the team used postgame debriefs and analyses to inform practices and identify areas to improve. The players learned their weaknesses and practiced to overcome them. They also built a powerful sense of cohesion.

But perhaps nowhere did the Leicester team better resemble a Vanguard unit than in its use of KPIs and metrics. Leicester tracked metrics other teams ignored, such as team cohesion, and as a result, the players gelled in a way their opponents didn't, allowing them to soar from last place in a lower league to first place in the top league in just two years.

ACHIEVE UNPARALLELED SUCCESS

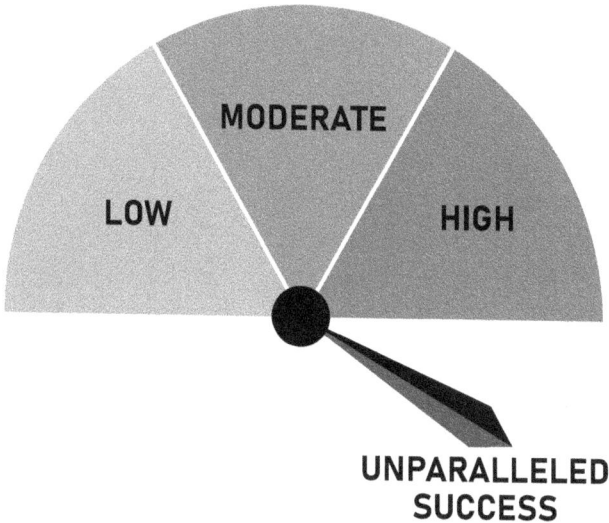

My goal in this chapter is to help you identify the metrics that make the most sense for your Vanguard team and ensure those metrics align with your organization's overarching goals. Great metrics drive continuous improvement. To help you achieve that, I'll give you some tools to help, including a metrics dashboard, a KPI selection guide, and methods for collecting feedback and insights that are sometimes quantitative and other times qualitative. The Vanguard Continuous Improvement

Framework (VCIF) I present here will help you take immediate action on what your metrics reveal. There is also a Team Cohesion Assessment that enables you to identify progress as well as areas of improvement, allowing you to pinpoint how to get better.

Metrics are the heartbeat of any successful team. Because they are an objective, factual representation of what has already happened, they provide clarity, direction, and a continually renewed sense of purpose. For leaders, they offer insights into team performance, areas of improvement, and potential growth opportunities. For team members, they provide a clear understanding of individual and collective contributions to the team's overarching goals.

The great challenge in measuring success is that it is often subjective. When I ask CEOs who their best people are—"Who on your team sets the world on fire in your organization?"—I often hear subjective assessments. "They light up a room," a leader will say about one team member. Or they'll say, "She's the hardest-working team member we have." These assessments sound great, but they aren't particularly helpful. I prefer objective measures. Remember, the second letter of the GOALS Model is that the success is "observable." For it to be a proper metric, people have to be able to see it.

When I press for specifics, it often makes people uncomfortable. But I've got a solution for that. The tools we'll introduce in this chapter allow you to quantify subjective qualities by assigning them to a 10-point Likert scale, giving you a quantitative score that lets you identify areas for improvement.

The Tools

Building a Vanguard team goes beyond setting goals. Taking a cue from Leicester City Football Club's success story, it's clear that tracking and refining those goals is crucial. That's where our tools come in. Whether it's a dashboard or a feedback system, each is designed to provide clarity, encourage improvement, and align with the Vanguard principles. These essential tools are the guiding force that helps teams achieve their best.

However, it's important to note that while these tools are carefully designed, they're also flexible. Every organization has unique challenges and goals, so each tool can be adjusted to fit your company's specific needs. For a more in-depth look and to access all the resources, templates, and guidelines, visit www.vanguardedge.com/resources. There, you'll find everything you need to support your Vanguard journey.

KPI Selection Guide

What is it?

A structured guide to help teams select the most relevant KPIs that align with their objectives and the broader company goals.

What are its key features?

It defines a KPI, differentiates it from a metric, and explains why KPIs are crucial to success. It uses a series of questions and a worksheet to help team members reflect on how their KPIs align with the team's mission, model, message, and GOALS. It also describes various types of KPIs, such as financial, customer, process, and people-oriented categories.

When to use it?

The selection guide is crucial when you set or reset the team's KPIs, or when the team is newly formed or undergoes a significant change. It's also a foundational resource during performance reviews and to ensure alignment when working with other teams or departments.

The Vanguard Metrics Dashboard (VMD)

What is it?

A comprehensive dashboard that transforms raw data into actionable insights. Whether you're using Excel, Google Sheets, or a more advanced data platform, this dashboard visualizes data using charts, color codes, and filters.

What are its key features?

The dashboard should include dynamic filters to focus on specific data, drill-down capability for a more detailed view of the data, and formatted cells to automatically calculate percentage changes, averages, or other metrics. Some teams will find it helpful to automate data entry, and the custom-view capability will allow team members to choose only those metrics they want to track. Tutorials on using the dashboard and input data will help bring everyone up to speed, particularly new team members.

An option for teams with more advanced resources is Tableau and Power BI, which can handle large datasets, provide mobile access, and include more automation options.

When to use it?

Use the VMD in weekly reviews, performance assessments, or any time you need a snapshot of team progress.

Vanguard Feedback and Insights Toolkit (VFIT)

What is it?

This resource empowers teams to collect quantitative and qualitative feedback, analyze it, and gain a holistic and nuanced view of their performance. It ensures you're equipped to make informed decisions.

What are its key features?

Integrated survey templates, focus group frameworks, interview techniques, and feedback analysis tools.

When to use it

Employ the toolkit during feedback-focused team workshops and strategic planning sessions. The toolkit helps ensure you are making data-informed decisions based on stakeholder feedback. The toolkit should be part of your continuous improvement efforts to align with stakeholder expectations and proactively address improvement areas.

Vanguard Continuous Improvement Framework (VCIF)

What is it?

The Vanguard Continuous Improvement Framework (VCIF) is a model designed to guide organizations through a structured process of growth and development, while remaining aligned with the team's mission, model, and message.

What are its key features?

The VCIF is built around six distinct stages. It begins with identifying opportunities or challenges that need attention. Next, there's a focus on planning the approach to address these areas. Once a plan is in place, strategies are implemented to bring about desired changes. As these strategies take effect, outcomes are closely monitored and analyzed to gauge their impact. Based on the insights gained, strategies are refined to better meet objectives. Finally, findings and insights are shared with the team to ensure everyone is aligned and informed.

When to use it

Use VCIF when aiming to systematically address and improve organizational processes or when seeking a structured approach to tackle specific challenges within a team or organization. It also works with project management, leadership training, and performance reviews.

Vanguard Metrics Workshop (VMW)

What is it?

This workshop dives deep into metrics, helping teams measure their success and develop a clear action plan for their metrics. Participants develop a holistic understanding of performance metrics through interactive exercises, collaborative discussions, and case studies.

What are its key features?

Metrics exploration exercises, collaborative discussions, real-world case studies, and action planning sessions.

When to use it

This workshop introduces new team members to metrics and aligns them with team KPIs. It's also useful as a quarterly checkpoint when the team revisits and refines its metrics and helps with metric alignment during broader strategic planning sessions.

Vanguard Team Cohesion Assessment

What is it?

This tool gauges a team's unity, alignment, and collaborative strength. It includes thirty statements that participants rank according to a 10-point Likert scale. It reveals a team's cohesion levels and identifies areas of strength and areas for improvement. Teams can use the assessment to improve their synergy and drive superior performance.

Scores in the "needs improvement" range may require workshops or other interventions.

What are its key features?

The assessment includes thirty statements, broken into six categories:

1. Communication,

2. Trust and respect

3. Collaboration and teamwork

4. Alignment and purpose

5. Conflict resolution

6. Support and recognition

Participants rank them from 1 (strongly disagree) to 10 (strongly agree).

The assessment provides category scores and an overall team score. The team score is prescriptive, showing you what action should be taken for the team (see Team Cohesion Score Sample graphic).

TEAM COHESION SCORE SAMPLE

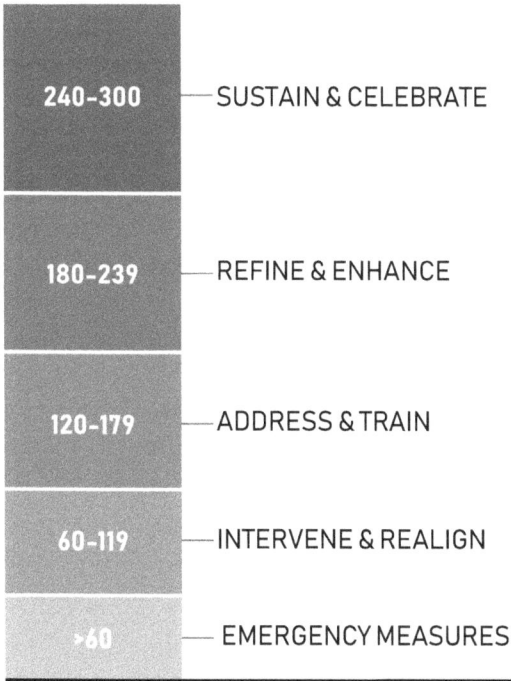

240–300	SUSTAIN & CELEBRATE
180–239	REFINE & ENHANCE
120–179	ADDRESS & TRAIN
60–119	INTERVENE & REALIGN
>60	EMERGENCY MEASURES

When to use it?

Quarterly, to track improvements or identify areas of concern.

Most Important KPIs

The most vital KPIs for measuring team success include the Team Cohesion Score, Project Completion Rate, Stakeholder Satisfaction, and Individual Contribution to Team Goals. These KPIs—derived from the KPI Selection Guide—stem from your work on the GOALS

Model. Remember, GOALS stands for growth-oriented, observable, action-driven, limit-crushing, and shared. When it comes to KPIs, the key elements of GOALS are observable, action-driven, and shared. These are the driving forces behind your KPIs.

Using the selection guide will ensure your KPIs are aligned with the growth objectives but are also observable, actionable, challenge the limits, and are shared among team members. Feedback loops and the Vanguard Continuous Improvement Framework (VCIF) emphasize rapid iteration based on metric feedback. This approach ensures that teams are agile, responsive, and quickly moving through the improvement process.

Team members should help set their own KPIs to give them a sense of responsibility and ownership. When KPIs are shared, the team performs better and engages more. Individual success is intricately tied to team success. By consistently revisiting the team's mindset, mission, and model, you can ensure your metrics are aligned and help drive those forward.

Team cohesion is one of the most important metrics, and we created the Vanguard Team Cohesion Assessment to measure how a team is performing. The tool uses thirty carefully curated statements from six categories—1) communication, 2) trust and respect, 3) collaboration and teamwork, 4) alignment and purpose, 5) conflict resolution, and 6) support and recognition. It asks members to rate the team on each using a 10-point Likert scale. By understanding their position on the cohesion spectrum, teams can enhance their synergy, improve collaboration, and drive superior performance.

We recommend a team cohesion analysis be done every quarter. This will allow you to track even the micro improvements and micro atrophy, giving you a sense of what the team needs to work on.

Tracking Progress

Utilizing regular retrospective meetings, progress-tracking technology, and team celebrations helps you ensure continuous progress. These tools help you understand pitfalls better and appreciate the intricacies of the team's journey.

Retrospective meetings are a critical part of this process. They allow teams to assess performance, identify what failed and what succeeded, and chart future steps. By fostering open feedback and using structured tools like the Vanguard Metrics Dashboard, teams can set clear action items and ensure continuous improvement.

Modern platforms like Tableau and Microsoft's Power BI allow real-time metric tracking, predictive analytics, and diverse data source integration. They give teams instantaneous performance views, allowing them to make fast, data-driven decisions. That you can plug in data and ask for analysis or predictive analytics is game-changing because the system will find mathematical patterns that the human brain can't detect, giving you a jump on addressing any problems that emerge. Tools like the

Vanguard Metrics Dashboard integrate seamlessly with existing platforms, allowing teams to monitor progress without interrupting their workflow.

Each team member should know where the entire team stands at all times. Remember, the S in GOALS stands for "shared." All goals are shared; everyone is on the same team. If you see a way to jump in and help a teammate achieve a KPI, you should. Individual successes add up to team success and vice versa.

When teams complete projects, hit target KPIs, or get positive stakeholder feedback, celebrations should be more than a pat on the back. Really celebrate. Celebrations boost morale, reinforce positive behaviors, and foster a culture of appreciation and recognition. Team members feel valued and are more motivated as a result. Small wins build confidence and motivation.

Some team members may balk at using metrics. Some don't think cold numbers are a good reflection of the work they do, some feel metrics promote competition rather than collaboration, and some don't like metrics because they struggle to achieve them. Whatever the resistance, leaders should approach it with empathy and education. Highlight stories like Leicester City's because they show how individual strengths, brought together as one team, can achieve greater things. Emphasize that metrics are tools to enhance team collaboration, not individual ratings.

When the metrics reveal an urgent problem, such as a decline in team cohesion, leaders should approach the problem with a solutions-oriented mindset. If interpersonal conflicts or misalignment are splintering the team, leaders can use tools like the Vanguard Feedback and Insights Toolkit to expose the root cause so they can address it. As always, foster open communication.

Along the same lines, leaders should ensure all data collection is transparent and collected with consent and security. Always get your team members' consent and invest in robust data security to protect privacy and the data's integrity.

Another concern is when leaders overemphasize metrics and foster a "numbers-only" mindset. The human aspects of teams are relegated to the back burner. Always remember to strike a balance: Metrics can guide decisions, but they should not dictate them at the expense of team well-being and the team's long-term vision. As a leader, it's vital that you avoid valuing quantity over quality.

A good example is when Wells Fargo came out with a company slogan that "Eight is Great." That meant the company's goal was to sell each customer eight products, such as a checking account, a debit card, an overdraft line of credit, a savings account, and so forth. The idea was to make the relationship as sticky as possible so people wouldn't switch banks. So if you wanted to continue to work for Wells Fargo and earn bonuses, you tried to sell each customer additional accounts. Before long, though, many employees started creating accounts for customers without the customers' knowledge or consent. When customers caught on, they objected, of course, and that led to regulatory scrutiny. After a short investigation from banking regulators, Wells Fargo was fined $185 million, the CEO and several other high-level executives resigned, employees were fired, bonuses were clawed back, and the reputation of the 170-year-old company was tarnished forever—all because their KPIs were misaligned with the company's values.

Chapter 5
Metrics Tools and Resources

Chapter 5 focuses on metrics, the critical aspect of quantifying and understanding your team's success. To guide you in this analytical journey, we introduce a suite of tools designed to measure, analyze, and enhance team performance:

1. Vanguard Continuous Improvement Framework (VCIF). This framework provides a structured approach to continuously assess and improve team performance, ensuring that your metrics are not just numbers but tools for ongoing development.

2. Team Cohesion Assessment. This assessment tool gauges the strength and effectiveness of your team's cohesion, which is vital for understanding the personal dynamics impacting performance.

3. KPI Selection Guide. This guide assists in choosing the most relevant and impactful key performance indicators (KPIs) for your team, aligning measurement with your specific goals and objectives.

4. Vanguard Metrics Dashboard (VMD). The VMD visually represents your team's performance metrics, allowing for easy tracking and analysis of progress over time.

5. Vanguard Metrics Workshop (VMW). An interactive workshop designed to help your team understand, embrace, and utilize metrics in their daily operations and decision-making processes.

6. Vanguard Feedback and Insights Toolkit (VFIT). This toolkit provides strategies for gathering and interpreting feedback, turning insights into actionable improvements.

7. Vanguard Team Cohesion Assessment. A comprehensive tool to evaluate the unity and effectiveness of your team, crucial for understanding how well your team works together towards common goals.

Each of these tools is crafted to give you a deeper understanding of your team's performance and areas for improvement. To access these tools, visit our online resource center at www.vanguardedge.com/resources.

Embrace these resources to measure, understand, and enhance your team's success, turning data into actionable insights.

Chapter 6

Multipliers: Magnifying Outcomes

....

*Give me a lever long enough and a fulcrum on which
to place it, and I shall move the world.*
—Archimedes

....

Adobe makes complex software for a range of creative professionals, from photographers and filmmakers to website builders and graphic designers. In fact, creative types often use several packages in their work. They edit photos in Adobe Photoshop, design graphics in Adobe Illustrator, and create their layouts in Adobe InDesign.

For years, Adobe sold its expensive software as individual, stand-alone products. InDesign users would purchase and load the software on their computers through floppy disks or CDs. Many would also buy and load Photoshop, Illustrator, and Premier, the video-editing software. Each year, Adobe would roll out updated and improved versions, forcing customers to purchase and load the software all over again.

Then, in 2012, Adobe switched from selling priority-licensed software to a software-as-a-service (SaaS) model. Instead of buying new editions of the software, users could subscribe to the Adobe Creative Suite, now called Creative Cloud, and pay a monthly or annual fee. Instead of purchasing and loading CDs, customers could now just click an icon and have software improvements automatically loaded on their computers as engineers released them. No more waiting eighteen months for the next software version to arrive in stores.

By 2017, Adobe's recurring revenue from subscriptions was **86** percent of the company's revenue. Its stock price rose 1,300 percent. By 2020, Adobe's revenue run rate grew from $4 billion in 2012 to an estimated $14 billion. Moreover, Adobe's bold move to a subscription model led the charge for other software companies to adopt the SaaS model. Today, **84** percent of net new software is delivered as SaaS products.

Adobe's shift to a subscription model is an example of the sixth M—multiplier. A business multiplier is anything that doesn't substantially increase the cost of your product but substantially increases your profits and effectiveness. The multiplier mindset is rooted in innovation, collaboration, and the pursuit of excellence. One type of multiplier comes from creating high-value offerings, and this is what Adobe did with its Creative Cloud.

Everything we've talked about so far has been about building a Vanguard team. You've adopted the right *mindset*, you've established your *mission*, and you've learned how to *model* a high-achieving and highly effective team. You've learned how to develop a *message* and a voice for your team, and you've designed the appropriate *metrics* to measure progress and maintain alignment for your Vanguard team. This chapter is a bonus chapter. This chapter outlines how you take the first five Ms and apply a force *multiplier* to it to launch your success even further.

For teams, multipliers are strategic tools or approaches that magnify the team's output, efficiency, or impact. Like a force multiplier in physics, the effect of using the tool is greater than the sum of individual efforts. A multiplier doesn't just add; it amplifies. For a team, multipliers would include strategies that enhance collaboration, tools that streamline processes, or initiatives that expand the team's influence beyond its immediate environment.

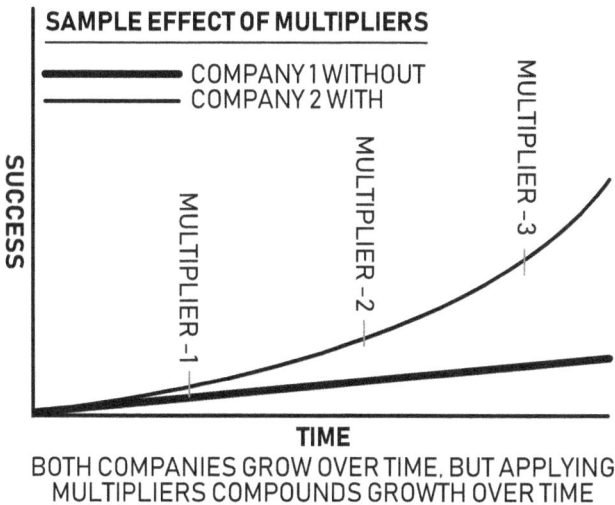

SAMPLE EFFECT OF MULTIPLIERS

COMPANY 1 WITHOUT
COMPANY 2 WITH

SUCCESS

MULTIPLIER - 1

MULTIPLIER - 2

MULTIPLIER - 3

TIME

BOTH COMPANIES GROW OVER TIME, BUT APPLYING MULTIPLIERS COMPOUNDS GROWTH OVER TIME

Types of Multipliers

Adobe's SaaS success is just one example of how to use a force multiplier. Here are a few others:

Strategic Partnerships

Some things just go together well. Peanut butter and jelly. Cookie dough and ice cream. Subaru and L.L. Bean. Nike and Apple. Starbucks and Barnes &Noble. Red Bull and GoPro.

Strategic partnerships make sense when you're already doing something well and making money. You form an alliance with another company with an adjacent product or a similar marketing list, and you do something in partnership with them. The goal is to amplify both companies' brands without adding significant costs, because you're both already spending money on it.

For example, if I market one type of product, and you market another type, and those products can be used together, why don't we market them together with one marketing budget?

Sometimes, strategic partners come up with an all-new product, such as when Target aligned with the high-end Lilly Pulitzer fashion brand on a line of affordable attire sold only in Target stores. The partnership opened new markets for Pulitzer and gave Target a valuable new product to market. The first release sold out within hours.

The same thing occurred in the 1980s in the aerospace industry when defense companies partnered to create products and then formed a joint venture that lived separately from the original two companies. Lockheed Martin is one example of that. Lockheed and Martin Marietta's ability to do things was multiplied when the companies combined.

For Vanguard teams, strategic partnerships allow teams to tap into wider networks and resources, amplifying their brand and offerings.

Networking Events

Networking events, such as conventions, seminars, or workshops, are a way to showcase your team's expertise and facilitate interactions with potential clients. It's a face-to-face way to build relationships. It's also efficient; you can often talk to a hundred people in the same time it would take you to have a one-to-one meeting with one customer.

For Vanguard teams, these events provide platforms for showcasing team expertise and forging new connections.

Experience Marketing

Another great strategy involves "experience marketing." Vanguard teams can offer immersive experiences that deepen stakeholder engagement. These can include interactive demos, workshops, or site visits that showcase the team's processes, culture, and results.

Referral Incentives

Your customers likely know people who would benefit from your product or services. So you want to build a referral program for your company to market your offerings to other companies. You might say, "If you sell my product for me to your customers, I'll pay you a fee." Affiliate marketing like this can be a huge economic boost.

Really, it's your company saying, "Let me use your customer list. You have customers who are similar to ours. We're not competitors, so I'll pay you to market my company to your customers." This helps Vanguard teams expand their reach without traditional marketing costs.

High-Value Offerings

Vanguard teams can create and market a special suite of high-end, high-value services that cater to an elite clientele. High-value offerings increase revenue as well as the value of your brand. And they act as a price anchor for your clients, meaning they may not buy the high-value offering, but that price point will help you sell lower price offerings at a higher price.

Memorable First Impressions

Apple, Tiffany, Louis Vuitton—these brands use packaging as a way of making great first impressions on their customers. The journey into their product begins when you hold the box, not when you flip the on switch. Apple led the way. The company designed elegant packaging. People videotaped themselves unboxing their new iPhone, put it online, and people watched those videos. They wanted to see what it was like to open those boxes. It created a ripple effect that elevated Apple's reputation and brand beyond its actual electronic products. Customers keep those boxes because they have some kind of intrinsic value, some inherent appeal. Louis Vuitton, Tiffany's, and Christian Dior boxes are found in households around the world because it feels almost sacrilegious to throw them away.

The Vanguard Team can use this multiplier by crafting unique and unforgettable first-contact experiences for potential clients or partners. This could be through personalized gifts, innovative presentation methods, or other creative gestures that leave an impression.

Community Engagement

Likewise, community engagements position the organization as responsible and community-minded. This could be through corporate social responsibility initiatives, sponsorships, or hosting community events. These multipliers drive organizational growth, foster a positive corporate culture, increase stakeholder trust, and provide valuable networking opportunities. Similarly, using "community" in a more digital sense, content collaborations allow you to team up with industry influencers, bloggers, or media outlets to co-create content, such as joint webinars and co-hosted podcasts.

Feedback Forums

These forums and roundtable discussions with clients, partners, and stakeholders provide valuable insights, foster stronger relationships, and position the Vanguard team as industry thought leaders.

Mentorship Programs

Senior members of the Vanguard team mentor people from other industries or organizations, establishing team members as experts, expanding external interactions, and providing potential business opportunities.

Real-Life Examples

Let's look at how some companies employed these practices to boost their business.

Airbnb

When the company first launched, people were a little suspicious. Homeowners didn't trust them, and neither did potential customers. You want me to host strangers? You want me to spend the night in some stranger's home?

To counter the distrust, Airbnb began having meetups—first in the big communities and then further and further out. The company invited both tenants and hosts to live events, where customers could see sample accommodations and meet hosts, and hosts could connect with the Airbnb mission in a way they couldn't through emails or browsing the company's website. Through this community engagement, Airbnb fostered loyalty on both sides. As hosts felt more connected to Airbnb's mission and each other, they became organic brand ambassadors.

It was grassroots experience marketing at its best. It brought Airbnb to the forefront, and it would not be the hospitality juggernaut it is today, if weren't for the multiplier effect of this community engagement.

Dropbox

Dropbox offered its existing clients free storage space when they referred people who became customers. At its peak, 60 percent of Dropbox's new users came through referrals from existing users. The multiplier effect was so significant that Dropbox dropped its advertising budget. The incentives turned existing users into active promoters, sparking exponential growth.

Tesla

Elon Musk's revolutionary car company faced resistance from buyers who worried about the range of the car battery and the availability of charging stations. They loved the cars but were reluctant to make longer trips where they might find themselves in unfamiliar territory with no way to charge their vehicles.

In response, Tesla introduced the Supercharger network—high-speed charging stations strategically located across major highways and cities. These stations alleviated "range anxiety" and offered a superior charging experience—fast, convenient, and exclusive to Tesla owners. The initiative emphasized Tesla's commitment to user experience, setting it apart from competitors.

Slack

The internal messaging service ran into some problems when potential customers balked at adding another layer to their IT ecosystem. The problem, the company learned, was that their product didn't integrate like Microsoft or Google Sheets did.

So the company opened its app to third-party developers and let them design plugins that allowed companies to fold Slack into their existing ecosystem. This allowed Google Drive, Trello, Salesforce, and other tools to seamlessly connect to Slack. These strategic partnerships gave Slack a huge boost. When customers could smoothly switch between products—even competing products—Slack became much more valuable, and adoption skyrocketed.

Finding Great Partners

The key to any multiplier is starting with a foundation that attracts partners. If you have a 1,000-person email list, you likely aren't going to get a partner with a 1-million-person list. You have to spend time becoming a great company so other great companies want to work with you. Exceptional companies can multiply their efforts because they can partner with many other exceptional companies. Building your team and your company starts with mastering the five Ms. Once you've done that, the sixth M becomes icing on the cake—that factor that allows your company to skyrocket.

If you have a Vanguard team in one industry, a multiplier might be the opportunity to meet and talk with a Vanguard team in a different industry. They have a common language and a common practice. They can share best practices, experiences, and innovations. In this sense, the two Vanguard teams can be a force multiplier for each other. They teach each other things you can find elsewhere, including this book!

It can also work with another Vanguard team from your own company. If you're on a product team, how could you multiply your efforts by working with a team from IT? How can the sales Vanguard team help and benefit from working with the customer feedback group?

Pinpointing the Right Multipliers

In choosing an appropriate force multiplier, teams must first determine if the multiplier directly supports the team's goals. If it doesn't fit your mission, it probably won't have the impact you're looking for. If it does support the mission, then you should remember that it also shouldn't add linear costs. If you're going to gain a thousand followers, it shouldn't cost you a thousand followers worth of money to achieve it. If it costs you ten followers to gain a thousand, then you might have a genuine multiplier in your hands.

An appropriate multiplier should also be feasible and scalable. For example, if your multiplier is to have the CEO network with every customer for two hours a month, it might make sense when you have ten customers. But what happens when you have two hundred? It's no longer feasible, and that multiplier is not scalable.

You also want to look at relevance—"Does that multiplier make sense for my product?"—and the cost-benefit ratio. Is the juice worth the squeeze? The return is not always money. A good multiplier could bring in more customers, enhance your brand, or improve your reputation. You've got to know what returns you're looking for, and you have to know how much it will cost.

Evaluating Multipliers

To determine if a multiplier is working, you must balance the potential returns against the investment. Take into account tangible benefits (more profit) as well as intangible benefits (brand enhancement). Carefully assess your investment, including financial costs, time, personnel, and other resources. Weigh potential risks before calculating your ROI.

There are some risks associated with multipliers. For example, you might become associated with a firm that drags you down instead of builds you up.

Multipliers can be found in unexpected associations. A good example is a beverage product called Liquid Death. It comes in a can that looks like a goth energy drink, and the label urges you to "murder your thirst." First, why would anyone buy a product named Liquid Death? And second, what are the ingredients?

Well, Liquid Death is nothing more than water, but it's purposely designed to look like one of those high-octane energy drinks, like Red Bull or Monster. The goal of that "contrarian" branding (water is actually the basis for life) was to piggyback on the heavy marketing work of energy drink brands. Energy drinks try to out-shock their competitors and have embedded in buyers' minds the understanding that the more outlandish the label, the greater the effect will be on your nervous system. Liquid Death founder Mike Cessario calculated that mimicking the energy drinks would make his water stand out in a crowded field and make it something people would buy regardless of what's in the can. It worked. Cessario is making millions off the idea.

Here's an excellent example of a multiplier having an outsized benefit on a team's performance: A tech startup introduced a referral program where they asked existing satisfied customers to bring in new customers. This team understood that people trust recommendations from friends and colleagues. Within six months, user signups tripled, and the team's per-customer acquisition costs dropped significantly. The team's brand ambassadors continued to expand the user base long after the referral program was launched.

Key Takeaways

- Multipliers amplify the work, expertise, and influence of your team. The impact is not just incidental; it can be exponential.

- Although some multipliers can be risky, they can also bring great rewards. They help your team spread its ideas and expertise, but they also help the team learn and compare notes with like-minded and highly functioning teams within and outside their organization. Your best strategic partners may not be the most obvious ones.

- The key is finding a partner you can help and who can help you in return. Whatever multiplier strategy you use, ensure that it fits your mission. Balance the investment with the returns, and be sure to include both tangible and intangible benefits in that assessment. Multipliers should not require a big investment, and they should be scalable and feasible.

Conclusion

Thriving, Not Just Suriving

....

The secret of change is to focus all of your energy not on fighting the old, but on building the new.
—Socrates (as quoted by Dan Millman in *Way of the Peaceful Warrior*)

....

Today's fast-changing business landscape requires companies and their teams to be agile, proactive, and resolute. The 6M Framework helps move teams from being risk-averse, siloed, reluctant, intractable, and in love with the status quo to being Vanguard teams that are forward-thinking, collaborative, open-minded, and ambitious. The framework helps teams embrace challenges and treat them as opportunities—a chance to learn and grow. It provides a way to measure success and continually improve.

The Vanguard Edge outlines how to make this journey by transforming your team into one with a growth mindset, where challenges are opportunities, mistakes have benefits, and continuous learning and adaptation are the norm. But changing mindset is just the start. The 6M Framework reshapes how your teams work by giving them a compelling mission; a robust model for the team that streamlines processes, enhances collaboration, and ensures harmony; clear messaging; strong metrics; and multipliers that amplify your work and lead to results that are not incremental but exponential. The **6M** Framework is a holistic approach. Each component works with the others, like gears in a finely tuned machine. When one gear moves, it sets the others in motion. When one gear improves, it enhances the function of the other gears.

While each "M" in the **6M** Framework is vital on its own, the synergy of the six cogs is what propels teams to Vanguard team success. It starts with the right mindset and flows from there. A growth mindset needs a well-defined mission, and a mission ensures the team's model, message, metrics, and multipliers are aligned and working toward a common goal. The model for the team's structure and strategy provides the blueprint to ensure the team is systematic and efficient in achieving its mission. The team's message—its voice to the world—clearly explains how the team is working toward its mission, ensuring the team is recognized, understood, and appreciated by its target audience. Metrics, a prerequisite for anyone with a growth mindset on a mission, provide insights, spotlight success, and identify areas for refinement. Multipliers, meanwhile, are catalysts that stem from the team's mission, model, message, and metrics. These are the tools and strategies that take a team's work from good to exceptional.

So you see, what we map here is a holistic approach. You can't cherry-pick what you think you need. You can't say, "We already have a good mindset and mission. We just need better messaging to be a Vanguard team." It doesn't work that way. Every team that goes through this must go through each step, in order. The things they discover during the implementation of each step will tell them they weren't ready for the thing they thought they needed.

How to Keep Evolving

The 6M Framework is a journey, but any Vanguard team must continue to evolve and move forward. That's just the way it is with teams that have a growth mindset, sound metrics, and a powerful sense of purpose. There's no place for complacency. Leaders can embed that mentality through:

- **Regular reflection and review**. Periodically reassess your team's current mindset, ensure the mission remains relevant, and evaluate the team model. This is particularly important if something in your environment has changed, such as new leadership, a shift in the organization's business strategy, or even a new team member. Ask yourself, "Do I need to refine communication strategies, analyze metrics for insights, and explore new multipliers?" This refinement process never stops. If you're the same team tomorrow that you were today, then you're not doing it right. If the metrics no longer make sense, don't wait until the end of the quarter to revise the metrics; revisit them immediately.

- **Embrace feedback**. Encourage feedback and foster a culture of valuing it. Regular input from team members, stakeholders, and customers can reveal framework elements that may need tweaking.

- **Continuous learning**. New research, tools, and strategies emerge regularly, so leaders should use seminars, workshops, courses, or reading to stay abreast of the latest in team-building and leadership.

- **Iterative improvements**. Instead of overhauling a framework based on a challenge or change, fine-tune specific components of the 6M Framework. Small, daily improvements compound and result in significant results in the end. Continuous learning leads to iteration.

- **Celebrate and reinforce successes**. Boost team morale and remind everyone of the framework's power by purposefully recognizing and celebrating milestones, big or small.

- **Stay connected with the community**. Engage with other leaders or teams implementing the 6M Framework. This engagement can provide fresh perspectives, insights, inspiration, and innovative ideas.

Leaders are catalysts for their teams' growth. For Vanguard teams, that means you are in tune with team members' needs, concerns, and aspirations. You listen more than you speak, and you ensure every voice is heard and valued. Here are some other tips for leaders:

- **Empower team members** to take ownership of their tasks. Trust your team's expertise and judgment. Give them the autonomy to make decisions.

- **Prioritize and invest in the continuous development** of the team through workshops, training sessions, and a culture of team knowledge-sharing.

- **Provide regular constructive feedback.** Don't wait for annual reviews to do this. Instead, celebrate successes and ensure feedback is specific, actionable, and delivered with empathy.

- **Maintain a transparent communication channel** to update team members about broader organizational goals, changes, or critical information. This transparency fosters trust and alignment.

- **Embody the values, work ethic, and attitude you want to see in your team.** This will inspire team members to emulate these behaviors.

- **Break down silos and encourage cross-functional collaboration.** Recognize that diverse perspectives lead to richer solutions.

- **Challenge team members** with new projects, roles, or responsibilities that align with their growth aspirations. Nudge them out of their comfort zones.

- **Use regular check-ins** to ensure team members are not overwhelmed, stressed, or facing personal challenges.

- **Celebrate big and small milestones.** Recognize individual and team contributions, which fuels a sense of belonging and value.

- **Encourage team members to voice new ideas, experiment, and learn from failures.** Promote a culture of innovation that ensures continuous growth and evolution.

Building the Skills

I've assembled a variety of tools on my website (www.vanguardedge.com/resources) to help leaders translate this book's theoretical overview into practical action steps. By weaving these tools into your daily operations, you can ensure the 6M principles are lived experiences, not theoretical concepts. In addition to the tools described in this book, here's a list of the types of tools you'll find on the website and when or how to use them.

- **Kick-off workshops.** During your first team workshop, use the **interactive worksheets** to help set the tone, introduce the 6M Framework, and align everyone's perspective. It's a hands-on way to brainstorm and lay down the foundational elements of each "M." The worksheets help teams brainstorm, plan, and implement the 6M Framework, from defining the mission to setting up metrics.

- **Regular check-ins.** During regular team meetings, use the **checklists** to address all aspects of the

6M Framework. These quick-reference checklists ensure that all key elements are being considered and addressed. A Vanguard team is an exciting thing, but it's also a tough thing for some people because there's a lot to it. Being a Vanguard team means you're a cut above. Expectations are high, and sometimes, that brings discomfort. Well-being check-ins are crucial.

- **Digital collaboration**. Implement the **digital templates** on platforms your team uses. We offer them for Microsoft Excel and Google Sheets, but if you have project management tools like Tableau or PowerBI, adapt the templates for those systems. Templates ensure that the 6M Framework becomes a part of the team's daily planning, tracking, and reporting.

- **Learning sessions**. Dedicate team meeting time to discuss real-world examples of each M. These discussions spark innovative ideas tailored to your team and provide insights into potential challenges and solutions.

- **Skill development**. When integrated into learning and development plans, the **video tutorials** ensure team members understand and apply the principles of the 6M Framework. They provide insights, tips, and innovations. Periodic **webinars** allow readers to interact with experts, ask questions, and learn from other teams using the 6M Framework.

- **Community engagement**. Promote active participation in the **community forums**. Sharing experiences, challenges, and successes with a broader community can provide fresh perspectives and solutions to common hurdles.

- **Feedback loops**. The **feedback mechanisms** ensure continuous improvement and alignment after major milestones or projects.

- **Resource days**. Dedicate time for the team to explore the **resource library**. This repository of articles, research papers, and other materials related to team building is constantly updated. Encourage team members to share interesting articles or insights, fostering a continuous learning culture.

- **Workshops**. Team members who attend our **exclusive workshops** gain in-depth knowledge and bring back fresh ideas and state-of-the-art practices to the rest of the team.

- **Integration with HR**. Collaborate with your human resources department to integrate these tools into onboarding, training, and performance reviews for your team, ensuring the 6M Framework is ingrained in the team's DNA. Say, your company spends time creating a vanguard team. There will be turnover. It's just natural. People move, and you'll have to hire somebody new. The new hire should be taught the framework as part of onboarding.

Getting Started

Keep in mind that the 6M Framework takes planning, patience, and practice. Don't expect to transform your team into a Vanguard team overnight. Leaders must be flexible and tailor implementation strategies to fit their teams. It's not a race, and even when the 6M principles are alive and well within your teams, the process is ongoing and requires vigilance. Here are a few ways you can start the journey and set the right pace:

- **Start with self-awareness**. You should first understand your team dynamics, strengths, and areas of improvement. This understanding will determine when interventions are most needed.

- **Implement the 6Ms in order**. Start with developing a growth mindset in your team and progress from there. You'll find that the Ms will emerge more quickly if you've taken the time to establish the previous one first. Some leaders may be tempted to implement the M they think needs the most attention, but establishing them in order makes the process more logical—and easier on your team.

- **Pilot programs**. Start with a beta group—such as one department or project team—before rolling out the framework on a broad scale. That initial group will help you see how quickly team members absorb the principles and will give you a sense of common potholes and how to avoid them. Top-down implementation works very well.

- **Engage champions**. Some team members are going to find it easy to adopt these principles. Take advantage of that. Identity and nurture champions within the team who can influence their peers and help establish the process. These champions can drive change, provide feedback, and ensure smoother adoption.

- **Regular check-ins**. As you phase in the Vanguard Model, schedule regular check-ins to assess progress, address concerns, and celebrate wins. This iterative feedback loop ensures that the team remains aligned and that potential issues are addressed promptly.

- **Leverage training and workshops**. Holding workshops focused on each M helps teams get in-depth knowledge and become proficient in one area before moving to the next.

- **Celebrate milestones**. Acknowledging wins boosts morale and reinforces commitment to the framework.

- **Iterative refinement**. Remember, the Vanguard Model is not a static framework. You don't just become a Vanguard team and stop using the tools. Instead, challenges will arise, and leaders should periodically revisit and refine their approach, particularly as team members and the market change.

- **Seek external insights**. Engage with industry peers, join forums, or seek a consultancy to gain fresh perspectives. Explaining your process to others helps you break the process down and improve your own work.

- **Stay updated**. Stay updated on team-building, leadership, and industry trends that hint at ways you can improve. Ensure the Vanguard Model remains innovative.

Challenges and Hurdles

Methodically and patiently introducing the 6M Framework ensures its successful adoption. But that's not to say you won't encounter delays and setbacks. If you anticipate these challenges, you'll be prepared to overcome them.

The most common hurdle leaders encounter is the team's resistance to change. Some team members will be uncomfortable with a new way of doing things. The best way to get them to engage in the process is by explaining the reasons for the change and involving team members in decision-making. When people know the "why," they'll help with the "how."

This 6M process uses a lot of tools—spreadsheets, matrices, workbooks, etc.—that can overwhelm people. So don't throw it all at them at once. You don't want change fatigue. Break implementation down into steps, and don't move ahead until everyone seems ready. As the leader, don't become so engrossed in the mechanics that you neglect the humans. This framework only works if you take the time to build relationships, trust, and excellent communication. Likewise, leaders need to lead this change patiently. You're all used to accomplishing things quickly and well—that's how you became leaders—but you can actually delay the process if you rush.

Here are a few more pitfalls and how to resolve them:

- **Vision misalignment.** Not every team member will understand the mission the same way. Again, take the time to get everyone on the same page. Spend meeting time periodically reviewing mission and strategy.

- **Inconsistency.** You want to regularly discuss and assess the 6M process. When a big job or challenge comes up, don't drop the process so everyone can scurry back to their silos and focus on the big challenge as they've always done. Stick with the plan. Make the time. Sporadic implementation leads to confusion, reduced efficacy, and doubt.

- **Insufficient resources.** Creating Vanguard teams takes time and resources for training and exploration. Leaders must plan their budgets accordingly and continually communicate the long-term benefits of investing in a program like this. If you have a high resource need and low resource capacity, you might spend two years rolling out the Vanguard team, while someone with more resources might roll out the Vanguard team over three or four months. It could be a longer journey, depending on how much you have. There's no hurry.

- **Fear of failure**. Even when you encourage risk-taking, some team members will worry about the repercussions of their mistakes. So you must encourage risk-taking and acknowledge failures as a vital element of the learning process you want your team to adopt.

- **Lack of accountability**. When workers leave their silos for cross-functional teams, they can feel understandably adrift. It's new territory. Their old ways of measuring success may not work anymore, which can lead to ambiguity about responsibility. The best solution to this problem is clearly defining roles and regularly checking on progress or delays.

- **External pressure**. Market dynamics, competition, and economic conditions can press down on your strategies and delay your progress. Acknowledge it when you see it happen, and try to remain agile and flexible. Adjust your Vanguard work as needed.

- **Neglecting feedback**. Feedback—good or bad—is a gold mine. Take feedback wherever you can get it—from team members, stakeholders, and clients. When you ignore feedback, you miss an opportunity to refine and grow.

- **Complacency**. Achieving initial milestones can be exhilarating, but leaders must guard against complacency. The journey to building a Vanguard Team is ongoing, and there's always room for growth, innovation, and improvement.

Get a Running Start

The best way to jumpstart your journey to a Vanguard team is through an immersive, three-day workshop. While this book provides a blueprint of the 6M Framework, the workshop offers personalized guidance dictated by your team's needs, interactive learning through role-playing and problem-solving exercises, and immediate feedback that accelerates the learning curve. What's more, your team has an opportunity to bond as it works toward common goals. An inherent accountability arises, and teams leave with knowledge, a renewed sense of purpose, and a drive to implement a holistic strategy for team excellence.

Before the workshop, we here at Mercury Performance Group assess the unique dynamics of your team so we can ensure the workshop's content and exercises are laser-focused on what you need. Your facilitators have studied high-performing teams and worked on them. They bring tons of experience, insights, and proven strategies. During the three days, you are freed from work responsibilities and daily distractions, allowing you to dive deeply into transformational activities.

You leave the workshop armed with actionable strategies, templates, and frameworks adaptable to various team scenarios you have back home. You are introduced to a platform for networking with peers from other organizations, and you receive ongoing support—such as follow-up sessions, resources, and consultations—that keep you on the right path.

You leave the workshop with a crystal-clear understanding of your team's mission and team members' roles. This clarity of purpose guides all decisions, actions, and initiatives. You also leave with strong team cohesion, and a better understanding of each team member's unique strengths. Over the three days, you'll also design a tangible action plan, a roadmap for the Vanguard team journey.

Here are a few more souvenirs from your workshop:

- **Elevated performance metrics**. These lead to measurable improvements in your team's performance indicators, such as increased productivity, enhanced innovation, or improved customer satisfaction scores.

- **A growth mindset.** This mindset that embraces challenges, learns from failures, and continuously seeks improvement is the bedrock of innovation and adaptability in a rapidly changing business landscape.

- **Mastery of effective communication.** Teams learn communication tools and techniques for open dialogue. They learn how to share ideas, feedback, and concerns constructively.

- **Empowerment through leadership**. Every team member is empowered to take on leadership roles in various capacities. This distributed leadership approach keeps the team agile and resilient.

- **Innovative problem-solving**. Teams learn to leverage collective intelligence and diverse viewpoints to devise innovative solutions.

- **Stakeholder engagement**. With a renewed focus on external interactions, teams learn to engage more effectively with stakeholders, from clients to partners, amplifying their reach and influence.

- **Sustainable growth blueprint**. Teams leave with a blueprint for sustained growth, equipped with tools to continuously assess, refine, and evolve their strategies.

Parting advice

As we close this chapter on building Vanguard teams, there are two essential pieces of wisdom I'd like every reader to carry forward:

- **People first**. At the heart of every Vanguard team are its members. Tools, strategies, and frameworks are vital, but it's the people who bring them to life. Invest in your team members, value their contributions, and foster an environment of trust, respect, and collaboration. When people feel valued and empowered, they go beyond, turning visions into reality. A team's true strength lies in its people, and by nurturing those relationships, you're laying the foundation for unparalleled success.

- **The power of persistence**. Building a Vanguard team is a journey filled with highs and lows, successes and setbacks. But every challenge you face is an opportunity for growth. The most successful teams aren't those who never faced obstacles, but those who persisted through them, learning and evolving at every turn. Embrace the journey, knowing that every step, no matter how difficult, brings you closer to that pinnacle of success.

Acknowledgments

Whether said by Aristotle, Euclid, Max Wertheimer, or some combination of them all (as ironic as that would be, given the saying), this book is a shining example of the phrase, "The whole is greater than the sum of its parts," especially when one of the parts is my brain.

I didn't create this work by myself. It is the work of many people who have shaped me as a person and leader over the years, as well as people who contributed directly to this text.

Rather than write pages of acknowledgments, "thank you" to those reading this who have been part of my years on this earth—family, friends, and co-workers—those who helped me become the leader and team builder I am today. I am forever grateful.

I want to specifically call out a few people who were instrumental in getting this book, its contents, and the companion website resources into your hands.

April Kerlew, thank you for encouraging me to finally move beyond "I'm going to write a book someday." And thank you for listening while I talked out ideas and tools, for reading notes and poking holes when needed, for proofreading first drafts, and for your support throughout the process. This book would not exist without you. You are a great friend and the Queen of Communications.

Mike Koenigs, thank you for encouraging me to think bigger—Gratitude = 11. I remember vividly standing on your balcony in La Jolla, CA, facing the ocean and cool January air, and promising you I would embrace the coming changes. The three days I spent with you and your Superpower Accelerator gave me the vision for this book and the courage to make it a reality. This book is a tribute to your work, *Your Next Act: The 6 Growth Accelerators for Creating a Business You'll Love For The Rest Of Your Life*. https://www.mikekoenigs.com/superpower-accelerator-go/

Eva Riihiluoma, thank you for keeping me on track during this process. I didn't know how vital a publishing director was until you. I like to set limit-crushing goals, and you never wavered in ensuring I stayed on task to achieve them. This book is finished because of you.

Leader's Press, thank you to the entire team for helping me learn and grow through this process—Alinka Rutkowska, Stephen Pamplin, Deborah Brannon, Marinel Balde, Annette Liwanag, Jim Sloan, and many others behind the scenes. I'm already excited about the next book!

And finally, thank you to my Mercury Performance Group Leadership Team, Amy Redmond, Brandy Deichert, Tearle Johnson, and Tony Lawrence. I am incredibly blessed to have you as my Vanguard team.

About Bryan Howard

Bryan Howard is a seasoned expert in human performance and organizational development, with a career spanning over two decades. Born in Polk County, Florida, and raised between Florida and Macon, Georgia, Bryan's journey is one of resilience and transformation. His mother, a resourceful single parent, instilled in him the values of hard work and determination, while his father, a Southern rock star, influenced his love for art and music.

Bryan holds a business degree from the University of Florida and a master's in instructional systems from Florida State University. His academic background is complemented by several executive coaching certifications and extensive leadership, team building, and human performance improvement training.

As the CEO of Mercury Performance Group LLC, Bryan has been instrumental in enhancing human performance for businesses across various industries, from start-ups to Fortune 50 companies. He has also held executive and senior leadership roles in human resources and business operations, leaving behind measurable, positive impacts in each position.

Bryan's philosophy revolves around his "5 Gs of Personal and Professional Success: Grit, Growth, Gratitude, Generosity, and Grace." These principles are the bedrock of his professional manifesto, emphasizing the importance of people-centric solutions, tailored strategies, and continuous learning for organizational success.

Beyond his professional life, Bryan resides with his wife, Erica, in Jacksonville, Florida. He avidly loves art, music, and theater and enjoys traveling to culturally diverse destinations. His love for wine and food, especially Italian wine, is one of his favorite indulgences. Bryan is also deeply committed to charitable work, serving on boards to help underprivileged children thrive.

In his professional and personal life, Bryan Howard exemplifies a commitment to excellence and a deep understanding of the human element in every endeavor. His work continues to inspire and transform, making him a pivotal figure in the field of human performance.

www.ingramcontent.com/pod-product-compliance
Lightning Source LLC
Chambersburg PA
CBHW040926210326
41597CB00030B/5199